SPANISH
PHRASEBOOK

I1048004

**GEDDES&
GROSSET**

Published 2008 by Geddes & Grosset,
David Dale House, New Lanark ML11 9DJ, Scotland

© 1998 Geddes & Grosset

First published 1998, reprinted 1999, 2000,
2001 (twice), 2002 (twice), 2003, 2004 (twice), 2005, 2008

ISBN 978 1 85534 350 4

Printed and bound in Poland

POLSKABOOK

CONTENTS

CONTENTS

CONTENTS

KEY TO PRONUNCIATION

Guide to Spanish pronunciation scheme

Vowels

a	between b<u>a</u>d and f<u>a</u>ther
ai, ay	as a in g<u>a</u>te
e	as in b<u>e</u>t
ee	as in s<u>ee</u>
eye	as in English <u>eye</u>
i	as in b<u>i</u>t
o	as in h<u>o</u>t
oo	as in p<u>oo</u>l
ow	as in h<u>ow</u>
u	is pronounced as w, as in swim
y	as in <u>y</u>acht

Consonants

c	(before e and i) sounds as <u>th</u> in <u>th</u>ank
h	is not pronounced
ñ	sounds as <u>ny</u> in ca<u>ny</u>on
z	sounds as <u>th</u> in <u>th</u>ank

Hyphens are given to show syllables but should be ignored when speaking. The stressed syllable in a word is in bold type.

GETTING STARTED

Everyday words and phrases

Yes
Sí
see

Yes, please
Sí, por favor
*see, por fa-**bor***

No
No
no

No, thank you
No, gracias
*no, **gra**-thee-as*

OK
Vale
***ba**-lay*

Please
Por favor
*por fa-**bor***

Thank you
Gracias
***gra**-thee-as*

Excuse me
¡Perdón!
*pair-**don***

Good
Bueno
***bway**-no*

I am very sorry
Lo siento mucho
*lo **syen**-to **moo**-cho*

Being understood

I do not speak Spanish
No hablo castellano
no a-blo kas-te-ya-no

I do not understand
No entiendo
no en-tyen-do

Can you find someone who speaks English?
¿Puede encontrar a alguien que hable inglés?
pwe-day en-kon-trar al-gee-en kay a-blay een-glays

Can you help me, please?
¿Puede ayudarme, por favor?
pwe-day a-yoo-dar-may, por fa-bor

It does not matter
No importa
no eem-por-ta

I do not mind
No me importa
no may eem-por-ta

Please repeat that slowly
Por favor repítame eso lentamente
por fa-bor, re-pee-ta-may e-so len-ta-men-tay

9

Greetings and exchanges

Hello
Hola
o-la

Hi
Hola
o-la

Good evening
Buenas tardes
*bway-nas **tar**-des*

Good morning
Buenos días
*bway-nos **dee**-as*

Good night
Buenas noches
*bway-nas **no**-ches*

Good-bye
Adiós
*a-dee-**os***

It is nice to meet you
Encantado / Encantada de conocerle
*en-kan-**ta**-do / en-kan-**ta**-da day ko-no-**thair**-lay*

How are you?
¿Qué tal estás?
kay tal es-tas

I am very well, thank you
Muy bien, gracias
mwee byen, gra-thee-as

It is good to see you
Me alegro de verlo
may a-le-gro day bair-lo

There are five of us
Somos cinco
so-mos theen-ko

This is — **my son**
  Este es — mi hijo
es-tay es — mee ee-ho

    — **my husband**
    — mi marido
    — *mee ma-ree-do*

This is — **my daughter**
  Ésta es — mi hwija
es-ta es — mee ee-ha

    — **my wife**
    — mi esposa
    — *mee es-po-sa*

11

Greetings and exchanges

My name is . . .
Me llamo . . .
may ya-mo . . .

What is your name?
¿Cómo te llamas?
ko-mo tay ya-mas

I am a student
Soy estudiante
soy es-too-dee-an-tay

I am on holiday
Estoy de vacaciones
es-toy day ba-ka-thyo-nes

I live in London
Vivo en Londres
bee-bo en lon-dres

You are very kind
Es usted muy amable
es oo-sted mwee a-ma-blay

You're welcome!
¡De nada!
day na-da!

See you soon
Hasta pronto
a-sta pron-to

Greetings and exchanges

I am from — America
Soy de — los Estados Unidos
soy day — *los es-ta-dos oo-nee-dos*

— **Australia**
— Australia
— *ow-stra-lee-a*

— **Britain**
— Gran Bretaña
— *gran bre-tan-ya*

— **Canada**
— Canadá
— *ka-na-da*

— **England**
— Inglaterra
— *een-gla-te-ra*

— **Ireland**
— Irlanda
— *eer-lan-da*

— **New Zealand**
— Nueva Zelanda
— *nway-ba the-lan-da*

— **Scotland**
— Escocia
— *es-ko-thee-a*

13

Common questions

— **South Africa**
— Sudáfrica
— *soo-da-free-ka*

— **Wales**
— Gales
— *ga-les*

Common questions

Where?
¿Dónde?
don-day

Where is...?
¿Dónde está...?
don-day es-ta...

Where are...?
¿Dónde están...?
don-day es-tan...

When?
¿Cuándo?
kwan-do

What?
¿Qué?
kay

How?
¿Cómo?
ko-mo

How much?
¿Cuánto?
kwan-to

Who?
¿Quién?
kee-en

Why?
¿Por qué?
por kay

Which?
¿Cuál?
kwal

14

How long will it take?
¿Cuánto tardará?
kwan-to tar-da-ra

How can I contact American Express / Diners Club?
¿Cómo puedo contactar la oficina de American Express/
Diners Club?
*ko-mo **pwe**-do kon-tak-**tar** la o-fee-**thee**-na day American
Express / Diners Club*

What is the problem?
¿Cuál es el problema?
*kwal es el pro-**blay**-ma*

Do you know a good restaurant?
¿Conoce algún buen restaurante?
*ko-**no**-thay al-**goon** bwen res-to-**ran**-tay*

Do you mind if I ... ?
¿Le importa que yo ... ?
*lay eem-**por**-ta kay yo ...*

What is wrong?
¿Qué ocurre?
*kay o-**koo**-ray*

What time do you close?
¿A qué hora cierran?
*a kay **o**-ra thee-**e**-ran*

Common questions

Where can I buy a postcard?
¿Dónde puedo comprar una postal?
don-day pwe-do kom-prar oo-na po-stal

Where can I buy currency?
¿Dónde puedo cambiar dinero en efectivo?
don-day pwe-do kam-byar dee-ne-ro en e-fek-tee-bo

Where can I change traveller's cheques?
¿Dónde puedo cambiar cheques de viaje?
don-day pwe-do kam-byar che-kays day bee-a-hay

Where can we sit down?
¿Dónde podemos sentarnos?
don-day po-day-mos sen-tar-nos

Where is the toilet?
¿Dónde están los servicios?
don-day es-tan los sair-bee-thee-os

Who did this?
¿Quién ha hecho esto?
kee-en a e-cho es-to

Who should I see about this?
¿Con quién debería hablar sobre esto?
kon kee-en de-be-ree-a a-blar so-bray es-to

Will you come also?
¿Va a venir usted también?
ba a be-neer oo-sted tam-byen

Asking the time

Spain is on GMT plus one hour in the winter and GMT plus two hours in the summer. The 24-hour clock is commonly used in Spain. *See also* Numbers, page 221.

What time is it?
¿Qué hora es?
kay o-ra es

It is — **nine-thirty pm (21:30)**
Son — las veintiuna trenta
son — *las bain-tee-oo-na trayn-ta*

— **six-fifteen pm (18:15)**
— las dieciocho quince
— *las dee-eth-ee-o-cho keen-thay*

— **a quarter past ten**
— las diez y cuarto
— *las dee-eth ee kwar-to*

— **a quarter to eleven**
— las once menos cuarto
— *las on-thay me-nos kwar-to*

— **after three o'clock**
— después de las tres
— *des-pwes day las tres*

17

Asking the time

— **nearly five o'clock**
— casi las cinco
— *ka-see las **theen**-co*

— **twenty-five past ten**
— las diez y veinticinco
— *las **dee**-eth ee bain-tee-**theen**-ko*

— **twenty-five to eleven**
— las once menos veinticinco
— *las **on**-thay **me**-nos bain-tee-**theen**-ko*

— **eleven o'clock**
— las once
— *las **on**-thay*

— **five past ten**
— las diez y cinco
— *las **dee**-eth ee **theen**-ko*

— **half past ten**
— las diez y media
— *las **dee**-eth ee **me**-dee-a*

— **five to eleven**
— las once menos cinco
— *las **on**-thay **me**-nos **theen**-ko*

— **ten o' clock**
— las diez
— *las **dee**-eth*

— **ten past ten**
— las diez y diez
— *las **dee**-eth ee **dee**-eth*

— **twenty past ten**
— las diez y veinte
— *las **dee**-eth ee **bain**-tay*

— **twenty to eleven**
— las once menos veinte
— *las **on**-thay **me**-nos **bain**-tay*

It is — **early**
Es — temprano
es — *tem-**pra**-no*

— **late**
— tarde
— ***tar**-day*

— **one o'clock**
— la una
— *la **oo**-na*

— **midday**
— mediodía
— *me-dee-o-**dee**-a*

— **midnight**
— medianoche
— *me-dee-a-**no**-chay*

19

Asking the time

at about one o'clock
sobre la una
*so-bray la **oo**-na*

at half past six
a las seis y media
*a las says ee **me**-dee-a*

at half past eight exactly
a las ocho y media en punto
*a las **o**-cho ee **me**-dee-a en **poon**-to*

in an hour's time
dentro de una hora
***den**-tro day **oo**-na **o**-ra*

in half an hour
dentro de media hora
***den**-tro day **me**-dee-a **o**-ra*

soon
pronto
***pron**-to*

this afternoon
esta tarde
*es-ta **tar**-day*

this evening
esta tarde
*es-ta **tar**-day*

this morning
por la mañana
por la man-ya-na

tonight
esta noche
es-ta no-chay

two hours ago
hace dos horas
a-thay dos o-ras

at night
por la noche
por la no-chay

Common problems

I am late
Voy con retraso
boy kon re-tra-so

I cannot find my driving licence
No encuentro el permiso de conducir
no en-kwen-tro el per-mee-so day kon-doo-theer

I have dropped a contact lens
Se me ha caído una lentilla
say may a ka-ee-do oo-na len-tee-ya

21

Common problems

I have lost	— **my credit cards**
He perdido	— las tarjetas de crédito
*ay pair-**dee**-do*	— *las tar-**hay**-tas day **kre**-dee-to*

— **my key**
— la llave
— *la **ya**-bay*

— **my traveller's cheques**
— los cheques de viaje
— *los **che**-kays day bee-**a**-hay*

I have no currency
No tengo efectivo
*no **ten**-go e-fek-**tee**-bo*

I must see a lawyer
Tengo que hablar con un abogado
***ten**-go kay a-**blar** kon oon a-bo-**ga**-do*

My car has been stolen
Me han robado el coche
*may an ro-**ba**-do el **ko**-chay*

My handbag has been stolen
Me han robado el bolso
*may an ro-**ba**-do el **bol**-so*

My wallet has been stolen
Me han robado la cartera
*may an ro-**ba**-do la kar-**tair**-ra*

AT THE AIRPORT

Iberia is Spain's main airline, operating both international and domestic flights. They have several direct flights daily from London Heathrow and Gatwick to Madrid and from London Heathrow to Barcelona. There are also flights from Heathrow to a total of thirty destinations, including Bilbao, Alicante, Granada, Gran Canaria, Málaga, Palma, Seville, Tenerife and Valencia. Iberia also operate flights from Manchester to Madrid and Barcelona, plus Alicante, Bilbao, Seville, Valencia and a number of other destinations.

British Airways run daily flights to Madrid and Barcelona from Heathrow as well as a daily flight to Madrid and six flights a week to Barcelona from Gatwick. Other BA services include a daily flight from Gatwick to Málaga, three flights a week from Gatwick to Jerez, and a twice-weekly flight from Heathrow.

Popular holiday destinations are served by charter airlines. Cheap flight-only tickets are available from tour operators.

Arrival

Here is my passport
Aquí está mi pasaporte
*a-**kee** es-**ta** mee pa-sa-**por**-tay*

AT THE AIRPORT

Arrival

How long will this take?
¿Cuánto tardará esto?
kwan-to tar-da-ra es-to

I am attending a convention
Voy a asistir a un congreso
boy a a-see-steer a oon kon-gre-so

I am here on business
Estoy aquí en viaje de negocios
es-toy a-kee en bee-a-hay day ne-go-thee-os

I will be staying here for eight weeks
Me quedaré aquí ocho semanas
may kay-da-ray a-kee o-cho se-ma-nas

We are visiting friends
Estamos visitando a amigos
es-ta-mos bee-see-tan-do a-mee-gos

We have a joint passport
Tenemos un pasaporte familiar
te-nay-mos oon pa-sa-por-tay fa-mee-lyar

How much do I have to pay?
¿Cuánto tengo que pagar?
kwan-to ten-go kay pa-gar

I have nothing to declare
No tengo nada que declarar
no ten-go na-da kay de-kla-rar

24

I have the usual allowances
Tengo los artículos permitidos
*ten-go los ar-**tee**-koo-los pair-mee-**tee**-dos*

This is for my own use
Esto es para mi uso personal
*es-to es **pa**-ra mee **oo**-so pair-so-**nal***

Common problems and requests

Can I upgrade to first class?
¿Puedo cambiar mi billete a primera clase?
*pway-do kam-**byar** mee bee-ye-tay a pree-**me**-ra **kla**-say*

I have lost my ticket
He perdido el billete
*ay pair-**dee**-do el bee-**ye**-tay*

I have missed my connection
He perdido el vuelo de enlace
*ay pair-**dee**-do el **bway**-lo day en-**la**-thay*

Please give me back my passport
Devuélvame el pasaporte, por favor
*de-**bwel**-ba-may el pa-sa-**por**-tay, por fa-**bor***

The people who were to meet me have not arrived
No ha llegado la gente que iba a recibirme
*no a ye-**ga**-do la **hen**-tay kay **ee**-ba a re-thee-**beer**-may*

Common problems and requests

Where can I find the airline representative?
¿Dónde puedo encontrar al representante de la compañía
  aérea?
*don-day pwe-do en-kon-trar al re-pre-zen-tan-tay day la
  kom-pan-yee-a a-air-ay-a*

Where do I get the connecting flight to Santiago?
¿Dónde puedo enlazar con el vuelo a Santiago?
don-day pwe-do en-la-thar kon el bway-lo a san-tee-a-go

    Where is — the bar?
  ¿Dónde está — el bar?
don-day es-ta — el bar

        — the departure lounge?
        — la sala de embarque?
        — la sa-la day em-bar-kay

        — the information desk?
        — la oficina de información?
        — la o-fee-thee-na day een-for-ma-thyon

        — the transfer desk?
        — el mostrador de transbordos?
        — el mos-tra-dor day trans-bor-dos

    Where is — the toilet?
  ¿Dónde están — los servicios?
don-day es-tan — los sair-bee-thee-os

Is there a bus into town?
¿Hay autobús a la ciudad?
*eye ow-to-**boos** a la thee-oo-**dad***

How long will the delay be?
¿Cuánto se retrasará?
kwan**-to say re-tra-sa-**ra

I was delayed at the airport
Me entretuvieron en el aeropuerto
*may en-tray-too-**byair**-on en el a-air-o-**pwair**-to*

My flight was late
Mi vuelo se retrasó
*mee **bway**-lo say re-tra-**so***

I was held up at immigration
Me entretuvieron en el control de pasaportes
*may en-tray-too-**byair**-on en el kon-**trol** day pa-sa-**por**-tes*

Luggage

Where is the baggage from flight number . . . ?
¿Dónde están los equipajes del vuelo número . . . ?
***don**-day es-**tan** los e-kee-**pa**-hays del **bway**-lo **noo**-me-ro . . .*

I have lost my bag
He perdido la bolsa
*ay pair-**dee**-do la **bol**-sa*

Luggage

These bags are not mine
Estas bolsas no son mías
*es-tas **bol**-sas no son **mee**-as*

Are there any baggage trolleys?
¿Hay carritos de equipaje?
*eye ka-**ree**-tos day e-kee-**pa**-hay*

Can I have help with my bags?
¿Puedo obtener ayuda para llevar el equipaje?
*pwe-do ob-te-**nair** a-**yoo**-da pa-ra ye-**bar** el e-kee-**pa**-hay*

Is there any charge?
¿Hay que pagar algo?
*eye kay pa-**gar** al-go*

I will carry that myself
Esto lo llevaré yo mismo / misma
*es-to lo ye-ba-**ray** yo **miz**-mo / **miz**-ma*

My baggage has not arrived
No ha llegado mi equipaje
*no a ye-**ga**-do mee e-kee-**pa**-hay*

Where is my bag?
¿Dónde está mi bolsa?
*don-day es-**ta** mee **bol**-sa*

It is — a large suitcase
  Es — una maleta grande
  *es — **oo**-na ma-**lay**-ta **gran**-day*

28

— **a rucksack**
— una mochila
— *oo-na mo-chee-la*

— **a small bag**
— una bolsa pequeña
— *oo-na bol-sa pe-ken-ya*

No, do not put that on top
No, no ponga eso encima de todo
no, no pon-ga e-so en-thee-ma day to-do

Please take these bags to a taxi
Por favor lleve estas bolsas a un taxi
por fa-bor, ye-bay es-tas bol-sas a oon tak-see

Careful, the handle is broken
Cuidado, el mango está roto
kwee-da-do, el man-go es-ta ro-to

This package is fragile
Este paquete es frágil
es-tay pa-ke-tay es fra-heel

AT THE HOTEL

Hotels and hostales

Spain classifies all its hotels and similar accommodation with a star rating that reflects their facilities and amenities rather than the comfort or style of the individual establishments, so a tower block hotel could be rated with four stars and a fine old *hacienda* with the character and atmosphere that makes it uniquely Spanish may score only two or three stars, or even fewer. These are official government ratings and should be clearly displayed at the entrance with gold stars on a blue plaque. They should also appear on the standard tariff sheet, which must be displayed at reception.

Prices are generally quoted per room rather than per person and VAT (IVA) is added to the bill.

Accommodation is divided into several categories but for the purpose of ratings there are two main divisions – hotels and *hostales*. Hotels are star-rated on a one-to-five scale, although there are some hotels whose level of luxury is distinguished by a separate GL (*Gran Lujo*) rating.

Hostales (or pensions) are cheap hotels, rather like boarding houses, are rated on a one-to-three scale, ranging from fairly basic but mostly having a shower and some having a lavatory and bath to frugal with cold water.

The kind of accommodation is also classified and described by initials that precede the star rating. If an hotel or *hostal* does not have facilities for meals other than breakfast, it is described as a *residencia*. A place that provides apartment-like suites with self-catering facilities, together with many of the public facilities that you would expect of an hotel, is called an *aparthotel*.

The Spanish Tourist Office (*Oficina Nacional Española*), 57–58 St James's, London SW1A 1LD, can provide full lists of hotels and hostales.

Paradores

In 1926 the Marqués de Vega-Inclán, the Royal Tourist Commissioner to King Alfonso XIII, established the first of Spain's state-run hotels, Paradores. Now there are well over eighty hotels under the Paradores Nacionales banner. They offer an authentic taste of Spain, since many occupy historic buildings, including castles, palaces, monasteries and other buildings of interest. There are also many modern Paradores in the chain, and all the old ones are equipped with modern facilities.

They are liberally scattered throughout Spain, with the accent on places of outstanding natural beauty or of historical interest. Apart from the furnishings and decor being typically Spanish, the Paradores make a feature of regional specialities in their cuisine.

Reservations and enquiries

I am sorry I am late
Siento llegar tarde
syen-to ye-gar tar-day

I have a reservation
Tengo una reserva hecha
ten-go oo-na re-sair-ba ay-cha

I shall be staying until July 4th
Me quedaré hasta el cuatro de julio
may ke-da-ray a-sta el kwa-tro day hoo-lee-o

I want to stay for 5 nights
Quiero quedarme cinco noches
kee-e-ro ke-dar-may theen-ko no-ches

Do you have a double room with a bath?
¿Tiene una habitación doble con baño?
tee-e-nay oo-na a-bee-ta-thyon do-blay kon ban-yo

Do you have a room with twin beds and a shower?
¿Tiene una habitación con camas gemelas y ducha?
*tee-e-nay oo-na a-bee-ta-thyon kon ka-mas he-may-las ee
  doo-cha*

Do you have a single room?
¿Tiene una habitación individual?
tee-e-nay oo-na a-bee-ta-thyon een-dee-bee-dwal

Reservations and enquiries

I need — **a double room with a bed for a child**
Necesito — una habitación doble con una
cama para un niño
ne-the-see-to — *oo-na a-bee-ta-thyon do-blay kon oo-na
ka-ma pa-ra oon neen-yo*

— **a room with a double bed**
— una habitación con cama doble
— *oo-na a-bee-ta-thyon kon ka-ma do-blay*

— **a room with twin beds and bath**
— una habitación con camas gemelas y baño
— *oo-na a-bee-ta-thyon kon ka-mas
he-may-las ee ban-yo*

— **a single room**
— una habitación individual
— *oo-na a-bee-ta-thyon een-dee-bee-dwal*

— **a single room with a shower or bath**
— una habitación individual
con ducha o baño
— *oo-na a-bee-ta-thyon een-dee-bee-dwal
kon doo-cha o ban-yo*

How much is — **full board?**
¿Cuánto es — la pensión completa?
kwan-to es — *la pen-syon kom-play-ta*

— **half-board?**
— la media pensión?
— *la me-dee-a pen-syon*

Reservations and enquiries

How much is it per night?
¿Cuánto cuesta por noche?
kwan-to kwes-ta por no-chay

Does the price include room and breakfast?
¿Están incluidos en el precio la habitación y el desayuno?
*es-tan een-kloo-ee-dos en el pre-thee-o la a-bee-ta-thyon
ee el des-a-yoo-no*

Does the price include room and all meals?
¿Están incluidos en el precio la habitación y todas las
comidas?
*es-tan een-kloo-ee-dos en el pre-thee-o la a-bee-ta-thyon
ee to-das las ko-mee-das*

Does the price include room and dinner?
¿Están incluidos en el precio la habitación y la cena?
*es-tan een-kloo-ee-dos en el pre-thee-o la a-bee-ta-thyon
ee la thay-na*

Can we have adjoining rooms?
¿Nos puede dar habitaciones contiguas?
nos pwe-day dar a-bee-ta-thyo-nes kon-tee-gwas

Are there other children staying at the hotel?
¿Hay más niños hospedados en el hotel?
eye mas neen-yos os-pe-da-dos en el o-tel

Are there supervised activities for the children?
¿Hay actividades vigiladas para los niños?
eye ak-tee-bee-da-des bee-hee-la-das pa-ra los neen-yos

Reservations and enquiries

Can my son sleep in our room?
¿Puede dormir mi hijo en nuestra habitación?
pwe-day dor-meer mee ee-ho en nwes-tra a-bee-ta-thyon

Do you take traveller's cheques?
¿Acepta cheques de viaje?
a-thep-ta che-kays day bee-a-hay

Which floor is my room on?
¿En qué piso está mi habitación?
en kay pee-so es-ta mee a-bee-ta-thyon

Do you have a fax machine?
¿Tiene fax?
tee-e-nay faks

Do you have a laundry service?
¿Tienen servicio de lavandería?
tee-e-nen sair-bee-thee-o day la-ban-de-ree-a

Do you have a safe for valuables?
¿Tiene caja fuerte para objetos de valor?
tee-e-nay ka-ha fwair-tay pa-ra ob-he-tos day ba-lor

Do you have any English newspapers?
¿Tiene periódicos en inglés?
tee-e-nay pe-ree-o-dee-kos en een-gles

Do you have a car park?
¿Tienen aparcamiento?
tee-e-nen a-par-ka-myen-to

Reservations and enquiries

Do you have a cot for my baby?
¿Tiene una cuna para el bebé?
tee-e-nay oo-na coo-na pa-ra el be-bay

Do you have satellite TV?
¿Tiene antena parabólica?
tee-e-nay an-te-na pa-ra-bo-lee-ka

What is the voltage here?
¿Qué voltaje hay aquí?
kay bol-ta-hay eye a-kee

Is there — a casino?
  ¿Hay — casino?
    eye — ka-see-no

    — a hairdryer?
    — secador de pelo?
    — *se-ka-dor day pay-lo*

    — a lift?
    — ascensor?
    — *as-then-sor*

    — a minibar?
    — minibar?
    — *mee-nee-bar*

    — a sauna?
    — sauna?
    — *sow-na*

— **a swimming pool?**
— piscina?
— *pees-**thee**-na*

— **a telephone?**
— teléfono?
— *te-**le**-fo-no*

— **a television?**
— televisión?
— *te-lay-bee-**syon***

— **a trouser press?**
— plancha para pantalones?
— ***plan**-cha **pa**-ra pan-ta-**lo**-nes*

Is there a room service menu?
¿Hay menú para el servicio de habitaciones?
*eye me-**noo pa**-ra el sair-**bee**-thee-o day a-bee-ta-**thyo**-nes*

Is there a market in the town?
¿Hay algún mercado en la ciudad?
*eye al-**goon** mair-**ka**-do en la thee-oo-**dad***

Is there a Chinese restaurant?
¿Hay algún restaurante chino?
*eye al-**goon** re-sto-**ran**-tay **chee**-no*

Is there an Indian restaurant?
¿Hay algún restaurante indio?
*eye al-**goon** re-sto-**ran**-tay **een**-dee-o*

37

Reservations and enquiries

Is this a safe area?
¿Es ésta una zona segura?
es es-ta oo-na tho-na se-goo-ra

Where is the socket for my razor?
¿Dónde está el enchufe de la máquina de afeitar?
don-day es-ta el en-choo-fay day la ma-kee-nee-ya day a-fay-tar

Is the voltage 220 or 110?
¿Es el voltaje de doscientos veinte o de ciento diez?
es el bol-ta-hay day dos-thee-en-tos bain-tay o day thee-en-to dee-eth

What time does the hotel close?
¿A qué hora cierra el hotel?
a kay o-ra thee-e-ra el o-tel

What time does the restaurant close?
¿A qué hora cierra el restaurante?
a kay o-ra thee-e-ra el re-sto-ran-tay

When does the bar open?
¿Cuándo se abre el bar?
kwan-do say a-bray el bar

What time is — breakfast?
¿Á qué hora es — el desayuno?
a kay o-ra es — el des-a-yoo-no

— **dinner?**
— la cena
— *la **thay**-na*

— **lunch?**
— la comida?
— *la ko-**mee**-da*

Service

Can I charge this to my room?
¿Puede cargar esto a mi cuenta?
*pwe-day kar-**gar** es-to a mee **kwen**-ta*

Can I dial direct from my room?
¿Puedo marcar directamente desde mi habitación?
*pwe-do mar-**kar** dee-rek-ta-**men**-tay **dez**-day mee a-bee-ta-**thyon***

Can I have a newspaper?
¿Me da un periódico?
may da oon pe-ree-o-dee-ko

Can I have an outside line?
¿Me da línea, por favor?
*may da **lee**-nay-a, por fa-**bor***

Can I have my wallet from the safe?
¿Puedo sacar mi cartera de la caja fuerte?
*pwe-do sa-**kar** mee kar-**tair**-a day la **ka**-ha **fwair**-tay, por
fa-**bor***

Service

Can I have the bill please
¿Puede darme la factura, por favor?
*pwe-day **dar**-may la fak-**too**-ra, por fa-**bor***

Can I hire a portable telephone?
¿Puedo alquilar un teléfono portátil?
*pwe-do al-kee-**lar** oon te-**le**-fo-no por-**ta**-teel*

Can I make a telephone call from here?
¿Puedo hacer una llamada telefónica desde aquí?
*pwe-do a-**thair** oo-na ya-**ma**-da te-le-**fo**-nee-ka **dez**-day a-**kee***

Can I send this by courier?
¿Puedo enviar esto por mensajero?
*pwe-do en-**byar** es-to por men-sa-**hair**-o*

Can I use my charge card?
¿Puedo utilizar mi tarjeta de pago?
*pwe-do oo-tee-lee-**thar** mee tar-**hay**-ta day **pa**-go*

Can I use my personal computer here?
¿Puedo utilizar aquí mi ordenador personal?
*pwe-do oo-tee-lee-**thar** a-**kee** mee or-de-na-**dor** pair-so-**nal***

Can I use traveller's cheques?
¿Puedo utilizar cheques de viaje?
*pwe-do oo-tee-lee-**thar** che-kays day bee-a-**hay***

Can we have breakfast in our room, please?
¿Podemos desayunar en la habitación, por favor?
*po-**day**-mos des-a-yoo-**nar** en la a-bee-ta-**thyon**, por fa-**bor***

Can you recommend a good local restaurant?
¿Puede recomendar un buen restaurante cercano?
*pwe-day re-ko-men-**dar** oon bwen re-sto-**ran**-tay thair-**ka**-no*

I want to stay an extra night
Quiero quedarme una noche más
*kee-e-ro ke-**dar**-may **oo**-na **no**-chay mas*

Do I have to change rooms?
¿Tengo que cambiarme de habitación?
*ten-go kay kam-**byar** may day a-bee-ta-**thyon***

I need an early morning call
Necesito que me llame por la mañana temprano
*ne-the-**see**-to kay may **ya**-may por la man-**ya**-na tem-**pra**-no*

    I need — a razor
  Necesito — una maquinilla de afeitar
*ne-the-**see**-to — **oo**-na ma-kee-**nee**-ya day a-fay-**tar***

        — some soap
        — jabón
        *— ha-**bon***

        — some toilet paper
        — papel higiénico
        *— pa-**pel** ee-**hyen**-ee-ko*

        — some towels
        — toallas
        *— to-**a**-yas*

Service

I need to charge these batteries
Tengo que cargar estas pilas
*ten-go kay kar-**gar** es-tas **pee**-las*

I want to press these clothes
Quiero planchar esta ropa
*kee-e-ro plan-**char** es-ta **ro**-pa*

Is there a trouser press I can use?
¿Hay prensa para pantalones que pueda usar?
*eye **pren**-sa **pa**-ra pan-ta-**lo**-nes kay **pwe**-do oo-**sar***

Please fill the minibar
Por favor, llene el minibar
*por fa-**bor**, ye-nay el mee-nee-**bar***

Please leave the bags in the lobby
Por favor, deje las bolsas en el vestíbulo
*por fa-**bor**, **de**-hay las **bol**-sas en el bes-**tee**-boo-lo*

Please send this fax for me
Por favor, envie este fax de mi parte
*por fa-**bor**, en-**bee**-ay es-tay faks day mee **par**-tay*

Please turn the heating off
Apague la calefacción, por favor
*a-**pa**-gay la ka-le-fak-**thyon**, por fa-**bor***

Please, wake me at 7 o'clock in the morning
Por favor, llámeme a las siete de la mañana
*por fa-**bor**, **ya**-may-may a las see-e-tay day la man-**ya**-na*

Where can I send a fax?
¿Dónde puedo enviar un fax?
don-day pwe-do en-byar oon faks

    Can I have — my key, please?
  ¿Puede darme — mi llave, por favor?
pwe-day dar-may— mee ya-bay, por fa-bor

          — an ashtray?
          — un cenicero?
          — oon the-nee-thair-o

          — another blanket?
          — otra manta?
          — o-tra man-ta

          — another pillow?
          — otra almohada?
          — o-tra al-mo-a-da

          — some coat hangers?
          — algunas perchas?
          — al-goo-nas pair-chas

          — some notepaper?
          — papel de cartas?
          — pa-pel day kar-tas

Has my colleague arrived yet?
¿Ha llegado mi compañero?
a ye-ga-do mee kom-pan-ye-ro

Problems

I am expecting a fax
Estoy esperando un fax
*es-**toy** es-pe-**ran**-do oon faks*

My room number is 22
El número de mi habitación es el veintidós
*el **noo**-me-ro day mee a-bee-ta-**thyon** es el bain-tee-**dos***

Please can I leave a message?
¿Puedo dejar un mensaje, por favor?
*pwe-do de-**har** oon men-sa-hay, por fa-**bor***

Problems

Where is the manager?
¿Dónde está el gerente?
*don-day es-**ta** el he-**ren**-tay*

I cannot close the window
No puedo cerrar la ventana
*no **pwe**-do the-**rar** la ben-**ta**-na*

I cannot open the window
No puedo abrir la ventana
*no **pwe**-do a-**breer** la ben-**ta**-na*

The air conditioning is not working
No funciona el aire acondicionado
*no foon-**thyo**-na el **eye**-ray a-kon-dee-thyo-**na**-do*

The room key does not work
No funciona la llave de la habitación
no foon-thyo-na la ya-bay day la a-bee-ta-thyon

The bathroom is dirty
El cuarto de baño está sucio
el kwar-to day ban-yo es-ta soo-thyo

The heating is not working
No funciona la calefacción
no foon-thyo-na la ka-le-fak-thyon

The light is not working
No funciona la luz
no foon-thyo-na la looth

The room is not serviced
La habitación no está preparada
la a-bee-ta-thyon no es-ta pre-pa-ra-da

The room is too noisy
La habitación es demasiado ruidosa
la a-bee-ta-thyon es de-ma-sya-do roo-ee-do-so

There are no towels in the room
No hay toallas en la habitación
no eye to-a-yas en la a-bee-ta-thyon

There is no hot water
No hay agua caliente
no eye a-gwa ka-lee-en-tay

Checking out

There is no plug for the washbasin
No hay tapón en el lavabo
*no eye ta-**pon** en el la-**ba**-bo*

Checking out

I have to leave tomorrow
Tengo que irme mañana
***ten**-go kay **eer**-may man-**ya**-na*

We will be leaving early tomorrow
Nos iremos mañana temprano
*nos ee-**ray**-mos man-**ya**-na tem-**pra**-no*

Could you have my bags brought down?
¿Podría hacer que me bajen las bolsas?
*po-**dree**-a a-**thair** kay may **ba**-hen las **bol**-sas*

Could you order me a taxi?
¿Puede pedirme un taxi?
*pwe-day pe-**deer**-may oon **tak**-see*

Thank you, we enjoyed our stay
Gracias, hemos disfrutado de nuestra estancia
***gra**-thee-as, **ay**-mos dees-froo-**ta**-do day **nwes**-tra e-**stan**-
  thee-a*

OTHER ACCOMMODATION

Apart from hotels, hostales and paradores, other accommodation options in Spain include self-catering apartments (*aparthotels*) or villas, camping and hostelling. Many of the major tour operators have a self-catering programme of villas and apartment as well as hotel holidays, or you can book your own through the Spanish Tourist Office (*Oficina Nacional Española*), 57–58 St James's, London SW1A 1LD.

Self-catering

Self-catering has become a popular alternative to hotel accommodation in Spain. Most of what's on offer is modern, but standards can vary quite significantly. Although individual villas are available for rent through several tour operators, most of the self-catering accommodation available is in either apartments or small villas within a complex.

Most apartments will provide only basic cooking facilities. You should have enough crockery, cutlery, pots and utensils to see you through simple meals, but there are rarely any electrical gadgets to make life easier. Cookers may be little more than a couple of electric rings – don't assume that facilities such as ovens will be available.

Prices of self-catering packages generally depend on the

Renting a house

number of occupants staying in the apartment. It is common
to count sofa beds as sleeping space for two of your party.
On a two-week holiday this can make your apartment seem
cramped, so check how your party is going to be accommo-
dated.

Villa complexes, or *urbanizaciones*, can be found all along
the Mediterranean coasts as well as in the Balearic Islands
and in the Canary Islands. Although most are booked
through package arrangements, you may be able to arrange a
booking on the spot. Villa complexes are unlikely to accept a
booking of less than a week, but apartments and aparthotels
will often agree to shorter stays. In villas you may be asked
to pay a deposit on top of the rental charges. Charges usually
include services such as gas and electricity, but be sure to
confirm this. Maid service is usually provided only weekly,
but it is sometimes possible to arrange additional service and
also baby-sitting.

Renting a house

We have rented this villa
Hemos alquilado este chalé
ay-mos al-kee-la-do es-tay cha-lay

Here is our booking form
Aquí tiene nuestra reserva
a-kee tee-e-nay nwes-tra re-sair-ba

We need two sets of keys
Necesitamos dos juegos de llaves
*ne-the-see-**ta**-mos dos **hway**-gos day **ya**-bes*

Can I contact you on this number?
¿Puedo contactarle en este teléfono?
*pwe-do kon-tak-**tar**-lay en **es**-tay te-**le**-fo-no*

Where is the bathroom?
¿Dónde está el baño?
***don**-day es-**ta** el **ban**-yo*

How does this work?
¿Cómo funciona ésto?
***ko**-mo foon-**thyo**-na **es**-to*

I cannot open the shutters
No puedo abrir los postigos
*no **pwe**-do a-**breer** los po-**stee**-gos*

Can you send a repairman?
¿Puede enviar alguien a reparar?
pwe**-day en-**byar** **al**-gee-en a re-pa-**rar

Is the water heater working?
¿Funciona el calentador de agua?
*foon-**thyo**-na el ka-len-ta-**dor** day **a**-gwa*

Is the water safe to drink?
¿El agua es potable?
*el **a**-gwa es po-**ta**-blay*

Renting a house

Is there any spare bedding?
¿Hay ropa de cama de más?
*eye **ro**-pa day **ka**-ma day mas*

The cooker does not work
No funciona la cocina
*no foon-**thyo**-na la ko-**thee**-na*

The refrigerator does not work
No funciona el frigorífico
*no foon-**thyo**-na el free-go-**ree**-fee-ko*

The toilet is blocked
El inodoro está atascado
*el een-o-**do**-ro es-**ta** a-ta-**ska**-do*

There is a leak
Hay un escape
*eye oon es-**ka**-pay*

We do not have any water
No tenemos agua
*no te-**nay**-mos **a**-gwa*

When does the cleaner come?
¿Cuándo vienen a limpiar?
kwan**-do bee-e-nen a leem-**pyar

Where is the fuse box?
¿Dónde están los plomos?
***don**-day es-**tan** los **plo**-mos*

Where is the key for this door?
¿Dónde está la llave de esta puerta?
don-day es-*ta* la *ya*-bay day es-ta *pwair*-ta

Around the house

bath
baño
ban-yo

bathroom
cuarto de baño
kwar-to day *ban*-yo

bed
cama
ka-ma

brush
cepillo
the-*pee*-yo

can opener
abrelatas
a-bray-*la*-tas

chair
silla
see-ya

cooker
cocina
ko-*thee*-na

corkscrew
sacacorchos
sa-ka-*kor*-chos

cup
taza
ta-tha

fork
tenedor
te-ne-*dor*

glass
vaso
ba-so

inventory
inventario
een-ven-*ta*-ryo

51

Around the house

kitchen
cocina
ko-thee-na

sink
fregadero
fre-ga-dair-o

knife
cuchillo
koo-chee-yo

spoon
cuchara
coo-cha-ra

mirror
espejo
es-pe-ho

stove
estufa
es-too-fa

pan
sartén
sar-ten

table
mesa
may-sa

plate
plato
pla-to

tap
grifo
gree-fo

refrigerator
frigorífico
free-go-ree-fee-ko

toilet
inodoro
een-o-do-ro

rubbish
basura
ba-soo-ra

vacuum cleaner
aspirador
as-pee-ra-dor

sheet
sábana
sa-ba-na

washbasin
lavabo
la-ba-bo

Camping

With a coastal climate conducive to being out of doors for much of the day, it's not surprising that camping is popular on the Mediterranean coasts, which is where most of Spain's 700-plus camp sites are located, particularly in the north, on the Costa Brava and Costa Dorada. But camping isn't restricted to the mainland. There are sites on both the Balearic and Canary Islands. Most sites are open only during the summer months, but some of those in areas of more favourable climate are open all year round.

Camping in Spain is for the most part restricted to camp sites. All camp sites are rated in categories from one (first class) to three (third class), depending on the facilities and services provided. Category one is the top of the range – in addition to the basic facilities of showers, toilets and a laundry, there should be a shop on the site, selling general goods, and a public telephone.

You can expect some of the sites in the top two categories to have shade, but this may well be at a premium during the hotter months, when the shady spots will be snapped up first.

Many camp sites will have some sort of café or restaurant to give you a break from the barbecue. It's worth finding out exactly what catering there is, since it could be quite a walk to the nearest resort or village.

All sites should have a post box and first-aid facilities, and

Camping carnet

bottled gas (usually Camping Gas only) is available at all but
the most basic of places. Some of the better sites will have
recreational facilities, including swimming pools and tennis
courts. Very few camp sites have tents or equipment for hire.
Some will have holiday chalets and cabins to let.

Rates for camp sites are based on a 24-hour period, starting at midday. There are usually reductions available for
long stays.

The Spanish Tourist Office (*Oficina Nacional Española*),
57–58 St James's, London SW1A 1LD, can provide you
with information. It's worth booking in advance if you plan
to visit Spain during the busy summer months. Once in
Spain, the *Guía Oficial de Campings*, available in book-
shops, gives details of most sites, and local tourist offices
can give you information on the nearest sites.

Camping carnet

A camping carnet provides not only an alternative to your
passport as identity but also gives third-party insurance
cover. Many camp sites still prefer you to have a carnet, although you should no longer be refused entry, as was once
the case. They are available from both the AA and RAC.

Camping rough

You can camp on open ground, with the owner's permission,
but not in mountainous regions or on beaches. And there are
other rules: you are not allowed to camp within a kilometre

of a town or village, near a national monument or within 150 metres of a main road or a drinking water supply; camps are restricted to a maximum of three tents and no more than ten people; you are allowed to stay in any camp for a maximum of three days; campfires are not permitted within 200 metres of a main road. (Fire is a major risk during the dry summers, and extreme care should be taken.)

Taking a caravan

Taking a caravan across the Channel can be expensive. It is worthy studying closely the available options on the various ferry services and Le Shuttle. Most companies charge according to length, although some also consider the height. Surprisingly, some peak-time ferry sailings have cheap rates for caravans, and several companies provide a substantial discount on return bookings.

If you're planning on taking a caravan, bear in mind that roads can get very congested in the summer, particularly along the Mediterranean coast, and that crossing the wide central plateau in searing summer heat can be quite an ordeal. It's worth considering either a late spring or an early autumn break. Only some camp sites allow caravans, usually the bigger and more expensive ones.

Speed limits for cars towing caravans differ from the standard limits for cars. They are:

Built-up areas: 60 kph (37 mph)

Useful camping questions

Single lane: 70 kph (43 mph)
Dual carriageway: 80 kph (49 mph)
Motorways: 80 kph (49 mph)
Note that cars with caravans and trailers are charged approximately twice the toll of cars on motorways. Be sure to include your caravan or trailer in your Green Card arrangements before setting off.

Useful camping questions

Can we camp in your field?
¿Podemos acampar en su terreno?
*po-**day**-mos a-kam-**par** en soo te-**ray**-no*

Can we camp near here?
¿Podemos acampar cerca de aquí?
*po-**day**-mos a-kam-**par** **thair**-ka day a-**kee***

Please can we pitch our tent here?
¿Podríamos montar la tienda aquí?
*po-**dree**-a-mos mon-**tar** la tee-**en**-da a-**kee***

Can we park our caravan here?
¿Podemos aparcar la caravana aquí?
*po-**day**-mos a-par-**kar** la ka-ra-**ba**-na a-**kee***

Do I pay in advance?
¿Tengo que pagar de antemano?
*ten-go kay pa-**gar** day an-tay-**ma**-no*

Useful camping questions

Do I pay when I leave?
¿Tengo que pagar al salir?
ten-go kay pa-gar al sa-leer

Is there a more sheltered site?
¿Hay algún lugar más resguardado?
eye al-goon loo-gar mas res-gwar-da-do

Is there a restaurant or a shop on the site?
¿Hay alguna tienda o restaurante en el camping?
eye al-goo-na tee-en-da o re-sto-ran-tay en el kam-peen

Is there another camp site near there?
¿Hay algún otro camping cercano?
eye al-goon o-tro kam-peen thair-ka-no

Is this the drinking water?
¿Es ésta el agua potable?
es es-ta el a-gwa po-ta-blay

The site is very wet and muddy
El terreno está muy húmedo y lleno de barro
el te-ray-no es-ta mwee oo-me-do ee ye-no day ba-ro

Where are the toilets?
¿Dónde están los servicios?
don-day es-tan los sair-bee-thee-os

Where can I buy gas?
¿Dónde se puede comprar gas?
don-day say pwe-day com-prar gas

57

Around the camp site

Where can I have a shower?
¿Dónde puedo ducharme?
don-day *pwe*-do doo-*char*-may

Where can we wash our dishes?
¿Dónde podemos fregar los platos?
don-day po-*day*-mos fre-*gar* los *pla*-tos

Around the camp site

air mattress
colchoneta hinchable
kol-cho-*nay*-ta een-*cha*-blay

backpack
mochila
mo-*chee*-la

bottle-opener
abrebotellas
a-bray-bo-*te*-yas

bucket
balde
bal-day

camp bed
cama plegable
ka-ma ple-*ga*-blay

camp chair
silla plegable
see-ya ple-*ga*-blay

can-opener
abrelatas
a-bray-*la*-tas

candle
vela
bay-la

cup
taza
ta-tha

fire
fuego
fway-go

flashlight
linterna
*leen-**tair**-na*

fly sheet
toldo impermeable
***tol**-do eem-pair-may-**a**-blay*

folding table
mesa plegable
***may**-sa ple-**ga**-blay*

fork
tenedor
*te-ne-**dor***

frying pan
sartén
*sar-**ten***

ground sheet
suelo impermeable
***sway**-lo eem-pair-may-**a**-blay*

ground
suelo
***sway**-lo*

guy line
viento
*bee-**en**-to*

knife
cuchillo
*koo-**chee**-yo*

mallet
mazo
***ma**-tho*

matches
cerillas
*the-**ree**-yas*

pail
cubo
***koo**-bo*

penknife
navaja
*na-**ba**-ha*

plate
plato
***pla**-to*

rucksack
mochila
*mo-**chee**-la*

shelter
refugio
*re-foo-**hyo***

59

Hostelling

sleeping bag
saco de dormir
sa-ko day dor-meer

spoon
cuchara
koo-cha-ra

stove
hornilla
or-nee-ya

tent peg
clavija
kla-bee-ha

tent pole
mástil de tienda
ma-steel day tee-en-da

tent
tienda
tee-en-da

thermos flask
termo
tair-mo

torch
linterna
leen-tair-na

Hostelling

Most Spanish hostels belong to the Red Española de Albergues Juveniles (REAJ) and are listed in the annual directory published by Hostelling International. Rates vary dependng on the season and whether you are under 26. You do not always need a Hostelling International membership card, but may have to pay more without one. The address of REAJ is Calle José Ortega y Gasset 71, 28006 Madrid.

Is there a youth hostel near here?
¿Hay algún albergue juvenil cercano?
eye al-goon al-bair-gay hoo-be-neel thair-ka-no

Can we stay here five nights
¿Podemos quedarnos aquí cinco noches?
*po-**day**-mos ke-**dar**-nos a-**kee theen**-ko **no**-ches*

Can we stay until Sunday?
¿Podemos quedarnos hasta el domingo?
*po-**day**-mos ke-**dar**-nos **a**-sta el do-**meen**-go*

Here is my membership card
Aquí está mi tarjeta de socio
*a-**kee** es-**ta** mee tar-**hay**-ta day so-**thee**-o*

I do not have my card
No tengo mi tarjeta
*no **ten**-go mee tar-**hay**-ta*

Can I join here?
¿Puedo hacerme socio aquí?
pwe**-do a-**thair**-may so-thee-o a-**kee

Are you open during the day?
¿Está esto abierto durante el día?
*es-**ta** a-bee-**air**-to doo-**ran**-tay el **dee**-a*

Can I use the kitchen?
¿Puedo utilizar la cocina?
***pwe**-do oo-tee-lee-**thar** la ko-**thee**-na*

What time do you close?
¿A qué hora cierran?
*a kay **o**-ra thee-**e**-ran*

Childcare

Do you serve meals?
¿Sirven comidas?
seer-ben ko-*mee*-das

— to take away?
— para llevar?
— *pa*-ra ye-bar

Childcare

Can you warm this milk for me?
¿Puede calentarme esta leche?
pwe-day ka-len-*tar*-may *es*-ta *le*-chay

Do you have a high chair?
¿Tiene alguna silla alta?
tee-e-nay al-*goo*-na *see*-ya *al*-ta

Is there a baby-sitter?
¿Hay una canguro?
eye *oo*-na kan-*goo*-ro

Is there a cot for our baby?
¿Hay alguna cuna para nuestro bebé?
eye al-*goo*-na *coo*-na *pa*-ra *nwes*-tra be-*bay*

Is there a paddling pool?
¿Hay piscina para niños?
eye pees-*thee*-na *pa*-ra *neen*-yos

Is there a swimming pool?
¿Hay piscina?
*eye pees-**thee**-na*

Is there a swing park?
¿Hay parque de columpios?
*eye **par**-kay day ko-**loom**-pyos*

I am very sorry. That was very naughty of him
Lo siento mucho. Ha sido una travesura suya
*lo **syen**-to **moo**-cho. A **see**-do **oo**-na tra-be-**soo**-ra **soo**-ya*

It will not happen again
No volverá a ocurrir
*no bol-bair-**a** a o-koo-**reer***

How old is your daughter?
¿Cuántos años tiene su hija?
***kwan**-tos **an**-yos tee-e-nay soo **ee**-ha*

My daughter is 7 years old
Mi hija tiene siete años
*mee **ee**-ha tee-e-nay see-e-tay **an**-yos*

My son is 10 years old
Mi hijo tiene diez años
*mee **ee**-ho tee-e-nay **dee**-eth **an**-yos*

She goes to bed at nine o'clock
Se acuesta a las nueve
*say a-**kwe**-sta a las **nwe**-bay*

Childcare

We will be back in two hours
Volveremos dentro de dos horas
*bol-bair-**ay**-mos **den**-tro day dos **o**-ras*

Where can I buy some disposable nappies?
¿Dónde puedo comprar pañales desechables?
*don-day pwe-do kom-**prar** pan-**ya**-les des-e-**cha**-bles*

Where can I change the baby?
¿Dónde puedo cambiar al bebé?
*don-day pwe-do kam-**byar** al be-**bay***

Where can I feed my baby?
¿Dónde puedo dar de comer al bebé?
*don-day pwe-do dar day ko-**mair** al be-**bay***

GETTING AROUND

Opening hours

Local tourist offices vary widely but are usually open Monday to Friday from 9.00 or 10.00am until 1.00 or 2.00pm. They close for lunch and re-open at 4.30pm until 7.00pm.

Post offices (*oficinas de correos*) are open in the mornings and again from 5.00pm to 7.00pm Monday to Friday and on Saturday mornings. Stamps (*sellos*) are also available from tobacconists (*estancos*) and from hotels.

Banks are open Monday to Friday from 8.30am to 2.00pm and on Saturdays from 9.00am until 1.00pm.

Museums open usually at 9.00 or 10.00 am but close for lunch. Some (but not all) reopen in the late afternoon. Many are closed all day on Mondays.

Most offices, shops and museums are closed on public holidays (*see* page 228).

Asking for directions

Where is — the art gallery?
¿Dónde está — el museo de arte?
don-day es-ta — el moo-say-o day ar-tay

Asking for directions

> — **the post office?**
> — el correos?
> — *el ko-**ray**-os*

> — **the Tourist Information Service?**
> — la Oficina de Turismo?
> — *la o-fee-**thee**-na day too-**reez**-mo*

Can you tell me the way to the bus station?
¿Puede indicarme el camino a la estación de autobuses?
*pwe-day een-dee-**kar**-may el ka-**mee**-no a la e-sta-**thyon**
day ow-to-**boo**-ses*

I am lost
Estoy perdido / perdida
*es-**toy** pair-**dee**-do / pair-**dee**-da*

I am lost. How do I get to the Carlos Quinto Hotel?
Estoy perdido / perdida. ¿Cómo se llega al Hotel Carlos
Quinto?
*es-**toy** pair-**dee**-do / pair-**dee**-da. **Ko**-mo say **ye**-ga al o-**tel**
Kar-los **Keen**-to*

Can you show me on the map?
¿Puede indicarme en el mapa?
*pwe-day een-dee-**kar**-may en el **ma**-pa*

May I borrow your map?
¿Puede prestarme el mapa?
*pwe-day pre-**star**-may el **ma**-pa*

Asking for directions

We are looking for a restaurant
Estamos buscando un restaurante
*es-**ta**-mos boo-**skan**-do oon re-sto-**ran**-tay*

Where are the toilets?
¿Dónde están los servicios?
***don**-day es-**tan** los sair-bee-**thee**-os*

I am looking for the Tourist Information Office
Estoy buscando la Oficina de Turismo
*es-**toy** boo-**skan**-do la o-fee-**thee**-na day too-**reez**-mo*

I am trying to get to the market
Quiero ir al mercado
*kee-**e**-ro eer al mair-**ka**-do*

Can you walk there?
¿Se puede ir andando hasta allí?
*say **pwe**-day eer an-**dan**-do **a**-sta a-**yee***

Is it far?
¿Está lejos?
*es-**ta lay**-hos*

I want to go to the theatre
Quiero ir al teatro
*kee-**e**-ro eer al tay-**a**-tro*

Is there a bus that goes there?
¿Hay algún autobús que vaya allí?
*a-ee al-**goon** ow-to-**boos** kay ba-ya a-**yee***

Directions – by road

Where do I get a bus for the city centre?
¿Dónde puedo coger el autobús al centro de la ciudad?
don-day **pwe**-do ko-**hair** el ow-to-**boos** al **then**-tro day la
  thee-oo-**dad**

Is there a train that goes there?
¿Hay algún tren que vaya allí?
eye al-goon tren kay ba-ya a-yee

Directions – by road

Where does this road go to?
¿Adónde va esta carretera?
a-don-day ba es-ta ka-re-tair-a

Do I turn here for Jaca?
¿Tengo que girar aquí para Jaca?
ten-go kay hee-rar a-kee pa-ra ha-ka

How do I get onto the motorway?
¿Por dónde se entra a la autopista?
por don-day say en-tra a la ow-to-pee-sta

How far is it to Toledo?
¿Qué distancia hay a Toledo?
kay dee-stan-thee-a eye a to-lay-do

How long will it take to get there?
¿Cuánto se tarda en ir allí?
kwan-to say tar-da en eer a-yee

Directions – what you may hear

I am looking for the next exit
Busco la siguiente salida
boos-ko la see-gee-*en*-tay sa-*lee*-da

Is there a filling station near here?
¿Hay una gasolinera aquí cerca?
a-ee oo-na ga-so-lee-*nair*-a a-*kee thair*-ka

Is this the right way to the supermarket?
¿Es éste el camino al supermercado?
es es-tay el ka-*mee*-no al soo-pair-*mair*-*ka*-do

Which is the best route to Pamplona?
¿Cuál es la mejor carretera para Pamplona?
*kwal es la me-*hor* ka-re-*tair*-a *pa*-ra Pam-*plo*-na

Which is the fastest route?
¿Cuál es la carretera más rapida?
*kwal es la ka-re-*tair*-a mas *ra*-pee-da

Which road do I take to Segovia?
¿Qué carretera debo coger para Segovia?
*kay ka-re-*tair*-a *de*-bo ko-*hair* *pa*-ra se-*go*-bee-a

Directions – what you may hear

Vaya — hasta . . .
  by-a — a-sta . . .
You go — as far as . . .

Directions – what you may hear

— a la izquierda
— *a la eeth-kyair-da*
— left

— a la derecha
— *a la de-ray-cha*
— right

Vaya hacia . . .
by-a a-thya . . .
You go towards . . .

Está — en el cruce
es-ta — en el croo-thay
It is — at the crossroads

— a la vuelta de la esquina
— *a la bwel-ta day la es-kee-na*
— around the corner

— bajo el puente
— *ba-ho el pwen-tay*
— under the bridge

— después del semáforo
— *des-pwes del se-ma-fo-ro*
— after the traffic lights

— junto al cine
— *hoon-to al thee-nay*
— next to the cinema

Directions – what you may hear

— en el siguiente piso
— *en el see-gee-**en**-tay **pee**-so*
— on the next floor

— frente a la estación de ferrocarril
— ***fren**-tay a la es-ta-**thyon** day fe-ro-ka-**reel***
— opposite the railway station

— allí
— *a-**yee***
— over there

Atraviese la calle
*a-tra-bee-**ay**-say la **ka**-yay*
Cross the street

Siga las señales a . . .
***see**-ga las sen-**ya**-les a . . .*
Follow the signs for . . .

— el próximo cruce
— *el **prok**-see-mo **croo**-thay*
— the next junction

— la autopista
— *la ow-to-**pee**-sta*
— the motorway

— la plaza
— *la **pla**-tha*
— the square

71

Directions – what you may hear

Siga todo recto
see-ga to-do rek-to
Keep going straight ahead

Gire a la izquierda
hee-ray a la eeth-kyair-da
Turn left

Gire a la derecha
hee-ray a la de-ray-cha
Turn right

Tiene que dar la vuelta
tee-e-nay kay dar la bwel-ta
You have to go back

Coja la primera carretera a la derecha
ko-ha la pree-mair-a ka-re-tair-a a la de-ray-cha
Take the first road on the right

Coja la carretera de Simancas
ko-ha la ka-re-tair-a day see-man-kas
Take the road for Simancas

Coja la segunda carretera a la izquierda
ko-ha la se-goon-da ka-re-tair-a a la eeth-kyair-da
Take the second road on the left

Hiring a car

The large international car hire firms all operate in Spain as well as local companies, and there is a wide range of cars available at differing prices. In theory you will need an International Driving Permit or a European Union driving licence but in practice a driving licence from any major country is sufficient. The basic hire charge excludes third-party insurance, VAT (IVA) and collision damage waiver. You must be over 21 and have held a driving licence for at least two years. You will usually have to pay by credit card. It is often worth arranging car hire in advance through an international firm or a fly-drive deal.

I want to hire a car
Quiero alquilar un coche
*kee-**e**-ro al-kee-**lar** oon **ko**-chay*

I need it for 2 weeks
Lo quiero para dos semanas
*lo kee-**e**-ro **pa**-ra dos se-**ma**-nas*

Can I hire a car?
¿Es posible alquilar un coche?
*es po-**see**-blay al-kee-**lar** oon **ko**-chay*

Can I hire a car with an automatic gearbox?
¿Puedo alquilar un coche con cambio automático?
*pwe-do al-kee-**lar** oon **ko**-chay kon kam-**byo** ow-to-**ma**-tee-ko*

Hiring a car

Please explain the documents
Por favor, explíqueme los documentos
*por fa-**bor**, eks-**plee**-kay-may los do-koo-**men**-tos*

We will both be driving
Conduciremos los dos
kon-doo-thee-ray-mos los dos

Do you have — a large car?
    ¿Tiene — un coche grande?
    *tee-e-nay — oon **ko**-chay **gran**-day*

        — a smaller car?
        — un coche más pequeño?
        *— oon **ko**-chay mas pe-**ken**-yo*

        — an automatic?
        — un coche con cambio automático?
        *— oon **ko**-chay kon kam-**byo** ow-to-**ma**-tee-ko*

        — an estate car?
        — una furgoneta?
        *— **oo**-na foor-go-**nay**-ta*

I want to leave the car at the airport
Quiero dejar el coche en el aeropuerto
*kee-e-ro de-**har** el **ko**-chay en el a-air-o-**pwair**-to*

I would like to leave the car at the airport
Me gustaría dejar el coche en el aeropuerto
*may goo-sta-**ree**-a de-**har** el **ko**-chay en el a-air-o-**pwair**-to*

Hiring a car

Is there a charge per kilometre?
¿Se cobra el kilometraje?
*say **ko**-bra el kee-lo-me-**tra**-hay*

Must I return the car here?
¿Tengo que devolver el coche aquí?
ten**-go kay de-bol-**bair** el **ko**-chay a-**kee

Can I pay for insurance?
¿Puedo pagar un seguro?
***pwe**-do pa-**gar** oon se-**goo**-ro*

Do I have to pay a deposit?
¿Tengo que pagar algún depósito?
***ten**-go kay pa-**gar** oon de-**po**-zee-to*

How does the steering lock work?
¿Cómo funciona el antirrobo?
***ko**-mo foon-**thyo**-na el an-tee-**ro**-bo*

I would like a spare set of keys
Me gustaría tener un juego de llaves de repuesto
*may goo-sta-**ree**-a te-**nair** oon **hway**-go day **ya**-bes day re-**pwes**-to*

Where is reverse gear?
¿Dónde está la marcha atrás?
don**-day es-**ta** la **mar**-cha a-**tras

Where is the tool kit?
¿Dónde está la caja de herramientas?
***don**-day es-**ta** la **ka**-ha day e-ra-**myen**-tas*

By taxi

Please show me how to operate the lights
Por favor, enséñeme cómo manejar las luces
por fa-bor, en-sen-yay-may ko-mo ma-ne-har las loo-thes

Please show me how to operate the windscreen wipers
Por favor, enséñeme cómo manejar los limpiaparabrisas
por fa-bor, en-sen-yay-may ko-mo ma-ne-har los leem-pya-pa-ra-bree-sas

By taxi

Taxis are easy to find in major towns and resort areas. They are distinguished by a green light on top and/or by colouring – black or white, with a broad stripe on the side. In cities, taxis can be hailed in the street – they display a *libre* sign if available for hire. Rates are reasonable and normally metered. Agree the fare first when this is not the case.

Where can I get a taxi?
¿Dónde puedo tomar un taxi?
don-day pwe-do to-mar oon tak-see

Take me to the airport, please
Lléveme al aeropuerto, por favor
ye-bay-may al a-air-o-pwair-to, por fa-bor

The bus station, please
La estación de autobuses, por favor
la es-ta-thyon day ow-to-boo-ses, por fa-bor

Please show us around the town
Por favor, enséñenos la ciudad
*por fa-**bor**, en-**sen**-yay-nos la thee-oo-**dad***

Please take me to this address
Por favor, lléveme a esta dirección
*por fa-**bor**, ye-bay-may a **es**-ta dee-rek-**thyon***

Could you put the bags in the boot, please?
Puede meter las bolsas en el maletero, por favor
*pwe-day me-**tair** las **bol**-sas en el ma-le-te-ro, por fa-**bor***

Turn left, please
Gire a la izquierda, por favor
*hee-ray a la eeth-**kyair**-da, por fa-**bor***

Turn right, please
Gire a la derecha, por favor
*hee-ray a la de-**ray**-cha, por fa-**bor***

Wait for me please
Espéreme, por favor
*es-**pe**-ray-may, por fa-**bor***

Can you come back in one hour?
¿Puede volver dentro de una hora?
*pwe-day bol-**bair** den-tro day **oo**-na **o**-ra*

Please wait here for a few minutes
Por favor, espere aquí unos minutos
*por fa-**bor**, es-**pe**-ray a-**kee oo**-nos mee-**noo**-tos*

77

By taxi

Please, stop at the corner
Por favor, pare en la esquina
por fa-bor, pa-ray en la es-kee-na

Please, wait here
Espere aquí, por favor
es-pe-ray a-kee, por fa-bor

I am in a hurry
Tengo prisa
ten-go pree-sa

Please hurry, I am late
Dése prisa por favor, se me ha hecho tarde
day-say pree-sa por fa-bor, say may a e-cho tar-day

How much is it per kilometre?
¿Cuánto cuesta por kilómetro?
kwan-to kwes-ta por kee-lo-me-tro

How much is that, please?
¿Cuánto es eso, por favor?
kwan-to es e-so, por fa-bor

Keep the change
Quédese con el cambio
kay-day-say kon el kam-byo

By bus

All significant towns and villages are connected by bus services. They are cheap but slow.

Does this bus go to the castle?
¿Este autobús va al castillo?
es-tay ow-to-boos ba al ka-stee-yo

How frequent is the service?
¿Con qué frecuencia es el servicio?
kon kay fre-kwen-thee-a es el sair-bee-thee-o

What is the fare to the city centre?
¿Cuánto es al centro de la ciudad?
kwan-to es al then-tro day la thee-oo-dad

Where should I change?
¿Dónde tengo que cambiar?
don-day ten-go kay kam-byar

Which bus do I take for the football stadium?
¿Qué autobús tengo que coger para el estadio de fútbol?
kay ow-to-boos ten-go kay ko-hair pa-ra el es-ta-dee-o day foot-bol

Where do I get the bus for the airport?
¿Dónde puedo coger el autobús para el aeropuerto?
don-day pwe-do ko-hair el ow-to-boos pa-ra el a-air-o-pwair-to

By train

Will you tell me when to get off the bus?
¿Me dirá cuándo bajarme del autobús?
*may dee-**ra kwan**-do ba-**har**-may del ow-to-**boos***

When is the last bus?
¿Á que hora es el último autobús?
*a kay **o**-ra es el **ool**-tee-mo ow-to-**boos***

By train

Spain's national railway, RENFE, runs a variety of services that will deliver you to your destination at quite different speeds and levels of comfort.

At the top of the scale is the *Talgo* service, which operates between major cities, with links to France. They are fast, modern, air-conditioned trains. If you have time on your hands, less money or maybe just a sense of romance, there are cheaper and slower services. *Rápido* trains stop only at main stations and, despite their name, are not necessarily fast. The slowest trains of all, *Regionales*, travel between provinces within a region and never miss a stop.

Bookings on RENFE trains can be made through European Rail Travel Ltd and American Express. RENFE operates various discounts, including reductions for travel on Blue Days (*Días Azules*), which are over half the days of the year. If you are anticipating a lot of train travel, you can buy a *Tarjeta Turística*, which you can use for four to ten days' travel within a two-month period.

Inter-Rail cards for passengers under 26 are accepted on Spanish services. You will have to pay part of the fare on some trains, such as the Talgo service. The adult version of the Inter-Rail card is not accepted in Spain.

Car-carrying services operate between various Spanish cities under the name *Auto-Expreso*.

Can I buy a return ticket?
¿Puedo comprar un billete de ida y vuelta?
pwe-do kom-prar oon bee-ye-tay day ee-da ee bwel-ta

A return (round-trip ticket) to Barcelona, please
Un billete de ida y vuelta a Barcelona, por favor
oon bee-ye-tay day ee-da ee bwel-ta a bar-the-lo-na, por fa-bor

A return to Paris, first class
Un billete de ida y vuelta a París, en primera clase
oon bee-ye-tay day ee-da ee bwel-ta a pa-rees, en pree-mair-a kla-say

A single (one-way ticket) to Lisbon, please
Un billete de ida a Lisboa, por favor
oon bee-ye-tay day ee-da a leez-bo-a, por fa-bor

A smoking compartment, first class
Compartimento de fumadores, primera clase
kom-par-tee-men-to day foo-ma-do-res, pree-mair-a kla-say

By train

A non-smoking compartment, please
Compartimento de no fumadores, por favor
*kom-par-tee-**men**-to day no foo-ma-**do**-res, por fa-**bor***

Second class. A window seat, please
En segunda. Asiento de ventana, por favor
*en se-**goon**-da. a-**syen**-to day ben-**ta**-na, por fa-**bor***

Can I take my bicycle?
¿Puedo llevar mi bicicleta?
*pwe-do ye-**bar** mee bee-thee-**klay**-ta*

Is this the platform for Zaragoza?
¿Es éste el andén para Zaragoza?
*es **es**-te el an-**den pa**-ra tha-ra-**go**-tha*

What are the times of the trains to Paris?
¿Cuál es el horario de trenes para París?
*kwal es el o-**ra**-ree-o day **tre**-nes **pa**-ra pa-**rees***

How long do I have before my next train leaves?
¿Cuánto tiempo tengo antes de mi próximo tren?
***kwan**-to tee-**em**-po **ten**-go **an**-tes day mee **prok**-see-mo tren*

Where can I buy a ticket?
¿Dónde puedo comprar un billete?
***don**-day **pwe**-do kom-**prar** oon bee-**ye**-tay*

Where do I have to change?
¿Dónde tengo que cambiar?
don**-day **ten**-go kay kam-**byar

Where do I pick up my bags?
¿Dónde se recogen los equipajes?
don-day say re-ko-hen los e-kee-pa-hays

Can I check in my bags?
¿Puedo facturar el equipaje?
pwe-do fak-too-rar el e-kee-pa-hay

I want to leave these bags in the left-luggage
Quiero dejar estas bolsas en la consigna
kee-e-ro de-har es-tas bol-sas en la kon-seeg-na

How much is it per bag?
¿Cuánto es por cada bolsa?
kwan-to es por ka-da bol-sa

I shall pick them up this evening
Las recogeré esta tarde
las re-ko-hair-ay es-ta tar-day

I want to book a seat on the sleeper to Paris
Quiero reservar una plaza en coche-cama a París
kee-e-o re-sair-bar oo-na pla-tha en ko-chay-ka-ma a pa-rees

Is there — a left-luggage office?
¿Hay — consigna de equipajes?
eye — kon-seeg-na day e-kee-pa-hes

    — a buffet car (club car)?
    — coche bar?
    — ko-chay bar

By train

> — **a dining car?**
> — vagón restaurante?
> — *ba-**gon** re-sto-**ran**-tay*

> — **a restaurant on the train?**
> — coche restaurante en el tren?
> — *ko-chay re-sto-**ran**-tay en el tren*

Where is the departure board (listing)?
¿Dónde está el tablón de salidas?
don-day es-ta el ta-blon day sa-lee-das

What time does the train leave?
¿A qué hora sale el tren?
a kay o-ra sa-lay el tren

Do I have time to go shopping?
¿Tengo tiempo para ir de compras?
ten-go tee-em-po pa-ra eer day kom-pras

What time is the last train?
¿A qué hora es el último tren?
a kay o-ra es el ool-tee-mo tren

When is the next train to Seville?
¿Cuándo sale el siguiente tren para Sevilla?
kwan-do sa-lay el see-gee-en-tay tren pa-ra se-bee-ya

When is the next train to Valencia?
¿Cuándo es el siguiente tren para Valencia?
kwan-do sa-lay el see-gee-en-tay tren pa-ra ba-len-thee-a

Which platform do I go to?
¿A qué andén tengo que ir?
*a kay an-**den** ten-go kay eer*

Is this a through train?
¿Es éste un tren directo?
*es **es**-tay oon tren dee-**rek**-to*

Is this the Madrid train?
¿Es éste el tren de Madrid?
*es **es**-tay el tren day ma-**dreed***

Do we stop at Vigo?
¿Paramos en Vigo?
*pa-**ra**-mos en **bee**-go*

What time do we get to Burgos?
¿A qué hora llegamos a Burgos?
*a kay **o**-ra ye-**ga**-mos a **boor**-gos*

Are we at Durango yet?
¿Hemos llegado a Durango?
*ay-mos ye-**ga**-do a doo-**ran**-go*

Are we on time?
¿Llegaremos a la hora prevista?
*ye-ga-**ray**-mos a la **o**-ra pray-**bee**-sta*

Can you help me with my bags?
Puede ayudarme con el equipaje?
***pwe**-day a-yoo-**dar**-may kon el e-kee-**pa**-hay*

By train

Is this seat taken?
¿Está ocupado este asiento?
es-ta o-koo-pa-do es-tay a-syen-to

May I open the window?
¿Le importa si abro la ventana?
lay eem-por-ta see a-bro la ben-ta-na

My wife has my ticket
Mi esposa tiene mi billete
mee es-po-sa tee-e-nay mee bee-ye-tay

I have lost my ticket
He perdido el billete
ay pair-dee-do el bee-ye-tay

This is a non-smoking compartment
Éste es un compartimento de no fumadores
es-tay es oon kom-par-tee-men-to day no foo-ma-do-res

This is my seat
Éste es mi asiento
es-tay es mee a-syen-to

Where is the toilet?
¿Dónde está el servicio?
don-day es-ta el sair-bee-thee-o

Why have we stopped?
¿Por qué hemos parado?
por kay ay-mos pa-ra-do

DRIVING

Driving in Spain offers some rewarding experiences, with excellent touring country in regions as far apart as the Pyrenees and Andalucía. But you should pay particular attention to preparations. It is a big country, temperatures can be high and roads can be rough.

Standards of driving in Spain are not high, and it is important to expect unpredictable behaviour from other drivers. In country areas, expect the roads to be used by slow-moving vehicles without lights and farm animals.

Any long-distance continental trip implies the need for some preparations – adjusting headlights, fitting a GB plate, getting an insurance Green Card, and so on. For Spain there are some special needs.

Holders of a green UK licence must also have an International Drivers Permit (IDP). Pink EU licences are fully recognised.

In the event of a serious accident, you may be arrested and/or your car may be impounded. By taking a Bail Bond – a guarantee of a substantial cash payment if you abscond – you are more likely to avoid confinement. Bail Bonds are available from motoring organisations.

A spare set of light bulbs and a red warning triangle are obligatory. If you wear glasses, you must carry a spare set in the car. Carrying a first aid kit and a fire extinguisher is also

The roads

recommended. Basic spare parts are worth taking for cars of non-European origin.

Choosing which way you get to Spain is likely to depend on various factors, such as how much time you have, what sort of budget you are on, whether you want to include a tour of France, and how much of a problem will be presented by long periods of driving.

If you are going to Barcelona, for example, you could opt for 24 hours on the ferry from Plymouth to Santander followed by a 720-kilometre (450-mile drive). Taking a short Channel crossing or using Le Shuttle through the Channel Tunnel instead will leave you with 1375 kilometres (860 miles) to drive to your destination but probably at a lower total cost. For a compromise on cost and driving time, the Portsmouth-St Malo route would leave a little over 1120 kilometres (700 miles) to reach Barcelona.

The roads

Some main roads are dual carriageways but most are not. On the major routes, roads are usually in reasonable condition, although they can be narrow in places, and it is not uncommon to find abrupt corners at the end of long straight sections. Hazardous mountain roads have acute hairpin turns and do not necessarily have crash barriers. In some relatively undeveloped areas, even main roads can be slow going, with few opportunities for overtaking. Some busy roads have become notorious for accidents. The N340, which runs the length of the Mediterranean coast from Barcelona to the Costa del Sol, claims many lives each year.

Spain has relatively few motorways (*autopistas*). Motorways currently exist along the northern Costas of the Mediterranean coast, from the border to Alicante. On the Atlantic coast, motorways run from the French border to Bilbao and a little way inland to Burgos, and there is a motorway link from here across to Barcelona on the Mediterranean.

Most motorways are subject to tolls. These can be paid by cash or credit or debit card, which you put through a machine. Tolls, which can be heavy, can be avoided by looking for the *peaje* (toll) sign then finding an alternative road.

Motorway services, both for refuelling and refreshments, are fairly regularly distributed. You can expect to find them about every thirty to fifty kilometres. For assistance on the motorways, emergency phones are generally available every two kilometres.

If you need a map, Michelin publishes a map covering Spain and Portugal and six larger scale regional maps covering Spain. They are accurate, up-to-date and available both in the UK and in Spain.

The rules

- driving on the right – this is relatively easy to adapt to, but extra care is needed when joining a road in circumstances

The rules

that may encourage you to revert to UK habits – when joining a quiet road, say.

- priority to the right – in the absence of any other indications, priority at intersections is given to traffic coming from the right. Intersections where traffic on a minor road gives way to that on a major one normally have a 'Stop' or give-way sight, 'Ceda el paso'.
- speed limits – the standard limits for cars are:
  built-up areas – 50 kph (31 mph)
  single carriageways – 90 kph (56 mph)
  dual carriageways – 100 kph (62 mph)
  motorways – 120 kph (74 mph)
  If you are overtaking outside a built-up area, you can exceed the speed limit by a maximum of 20 kph (12 mph) to do so.
- the minimum age for driving in Spain is eighteen.
- overtaking outside built-up areas requires the use of the horn as well as indicators. In built-up areas, where horns may be used only in cases of emergency, you should flash your headlights.
- safety belts are obligatory, if fitted. Children should travel in the rear seats.
- as in the UK, spare petrol must be carried only in approved containers.
- use dipped headlights when driving in built-up areas.
- drink-driving is subject to the same blood-alcohol limit as in the UK.

• fines – Spanish police can, and do, levy on-the-spot fines.
  You can be fined for many offences – speeding, breaking
  traffic rules, failing to have a correct GB sticker, and so on.

Traffic and weather conditions

Are there any hold-ups?
¿Hay atascos?
*eye a-**tas**-kos*

Is the traffic heavy?
¿Hay mucho tráfico?
*eye **moo**-cho **tra**-fee-ko*

Is the traffic one-way?
¿Es sentido único?
*es sen-**tee**-do **oo**-nee-ko*

Is there a different way to the stadium?
¿Hay otro camino al estadio?
*eye **o**-tro ka-**mee**-no al es-**ta**-dee-o*

Is there a toll on this motorway (highway)?
¿Esta autopista es de peaje?
*es-ta ow-to-**pee**-sta es day pay-**a**-hay*

What is causing this traffic jam?
¿Qué está causando este embotellamiento?
*kay es-**ta** kow-**san**-do **es**-tay em-bo-te-ya-**myen**-to*

Traffic and weather conditions

What is the speed limit?
¿Cuál es el límite de velocidad?
*kwal es el **lee**-mee-tay day be-lo-thee-**dad***

What time does the car park close?
¿Cuándo se cierra el parking?
***kwan**-do say thee-**e**-ra el **par**-keen*

When is the rush hour?
¿Cuándo es la hora punta?
***kwan**-do es la **o**-ra **poon**-ta*

Do I need snow chains?
¿Necesito cadenas para la nieve?
*ne-the-**see**-to ka-**day**-nas **pa**-ra la nee-**e**-bay*

Is the pass open?
¿Está el paso abierto?
*es-**ta** el **pa**-so a-bee-**air**-to*

Is the road to Segovia snowed up?
¿Está nevada la carretera a Segovia?
*es-**ta** ne-**ba**-da la ka-re-**tair**-a a se-**go**-bee-a*

When will the road be clear?
¿Cuándo estará la carretera despejada?
***kwan**-do es-ta-**ra** la ka-re-**tair**-a des-pe-**ha**-da*

Parking

Parking is usually controlled by local signs. Always park the car facing in the direction of the traffic. Which side of a one-way street you may park depends on the house numbers and which day of the month it is. On even dates you should park on the even-numbered side of the street and conversely for odd dates. In a 'blue zone' (*zona azul*), parking requires a disc or ticket permits – usually obtainable from shops such as tobacconists or from hotels, and travel agencies – and is generally restricted to an hour and a half.

Is it safe to park here?
¿Es seguro aparcar aquí?
*es se-**goo**-ro a-par-**kar** a-**kee***

Can I park here?
¿Puedo aparcar aquí?
*pwe-do a-par-**kar** a-**kee***

Do I need a parking disc?
¿Necesito ficha de aparcamiento?
*ne-the-**see**-to **fee**-cha day a-par-ka-**myen**-to*

Where can I get a parking disc?
¿Dónde puedo obtener una ficha de aparcamiento?
***don**-day **pwe**-do ob-te-**nair oo**-na **fee**-cha day a-par-ka-**myen**-to*

At the service station

Where do I pay?
¿Dónde tengo que pagar?
don-day *ten*-go kay pa-*gar*

Where is there a car park (parking lot)?
¿Dónde hay un aparcamiento?
don-day *a-ee* oon a-par-ka-*myen*-to

How long can I stay here?
¿Cuánto tiempo puedo permanecer aquí?
kwan-to tee-*em*-po *pwe*-do pair-ma-ne-*thair* a-*kee*

   Do I need — coins for the meter?
   ¿Necesito — monedas para el parquímetro?
ne-the-see-to — mo-*nay*-das *pa*-ra el par-*kee*-me-tro

            — parking lights?
            — luces de posición?
            — *loo*-thes day po-zee-*thyon*

At the service station

If you plan on touring remote areas, it is worth topping up the tank whenever it gets down to a quarter full. Beware of fuel stations closing on public and religious holidays (*see* page 228). You may need to be quite resourceful to find fuel in that event. Sometimes marina fuel pumps can help out.

Spain employs petrol octane standards that closely match those used in the UK. 'Gasolina' or 'normal', which has an

At the service station

octane rating of 92, is equivalent to our 2-star. 'Súper', with an octane rating of 97, is the same as our 4-star. Unleaded petrol – 'gasolina sin plomo' – is widely available. Diesel fuel is called 'gasóleo'.

Do you take credit cards?
¿Acepta tarjetas de crédito?
a-thep-ta tar-hay-tas day kre-dee-to

Can you clean the windscreen?
¿Puede limpiar el parabrisas?
pwe-day leem-pyar el pa-ra-bree-sas

Fill the tank please
Llene el depósito, por favor
ye-nay el de-po-zee-to, por fa-bor

25 litres of — unleaded petrol
Veinticinco litros de — gasolina sin plomo
bain-tee-theen-ko lee-tros day — ga-so-lee-na seen plo-mo

— **2 star**
— normal
— *nor-mal*

— **4 star**
— súper
— *soo-pair*

— **diesel**
— gas-oil
— *ga-zoil*

Breakdowns and repairs

I need some distilled water
Necesito agua destilada
ne-the-see-to a-gwa de-stee-la-da

Check the tyre pressure, please
Revise la presión de los neumáticos, por favor
re-bee-say la pre-syon day los nay-oo-ma-tee-kos, por fa-bor

The pressure should be 2.3 at the front and 2.5 at the rear
La presión debería estar en dos coma tres en los delanteros
    y dos coma cinco en los traseros
*la pre-syon de-be-ree-a es-tar en dos ko-ma tres en los
    de-lan-tair-os ee dos ko-ma theen-ko en los tra-sair-os*

> **Check — the oil**
> Revise — el aceite
> *re-bee-say — el a-thay-ee-tay*
>
> **— the water**
> — el agua
> — *el a-gwa*

Breakdowns and repairs

If you take out some form of breakdown insurance, the documents you are given will explain how to get help if your car goes wrong. Otherwise you will probably need to find the nearest garage, although RACE (Real Automóvil Club de España, the Spanish Royal Automobile Club) has a break-

Breakdowns and repairs

down centre that members of foreign motoring organisations can use. On a motorway you should find an emergency phone about every two kilometres.

Can you give me — a push?
      ¿Puede — empujarme?
    *pwe-day — em-poo-**har**-may*

              — a tow?
              — remolcarme?
              *— re-mol-**kar**-may*

Can you send a recovery truck?
¿Puede enviar un camión grúa?
*pwe-day en-**byar** oon ka-**myon groo**-a*

Can you take me to the nearest garage?
¿Puede llevarme al garage más cercano?
*pwe-day ye-**bar**-may al ga-**ra**-hay mas thair-**ka**-no*

Is there a telephone nearby?
¿Hay algún teléfono cercano?
*a-ee al-**goon** te-**le**-fo-no thair-**ka**-no*

Can you find out what the trouble is?
¿Puede encontrar el problema?
*pwe-day en-kon-**trar** el pro-**blay**-ma*

Can you give me a can of petrol, please?
¿Me da un bidón de gasolina, por favor?
*may da oon bee-**don** day ga-so-**lee**-na, por fa-**bor***

Breakdowns and repairs

Can you repair a flat tyre?
¿Puede reparar una rueda desinflada?
*pwe-day re-pa-**rar** **oo**-na roo-**ay**-da des-een-**fla**-da*

Can you repair it for the time being?
¿Puede repararlo provisionalmente?
*pwe-day re-pa-**rar**-lo pro-bees-yo-nal-**men**-tay*

Can you replace the windscreen wiper blades?
¿Puede cambiar las paletas del limpiaparabrisas?
*pwe-day kam-**byar** las pa-**lay**-tas del leem-pya-pa-ra-**bree**-sas*

My car has broken down
Mi coche se ha averiado
*mee **ko**-chay say a a-be-ree-**a**-do*

My car will not start
Mi coche no arranca
*mee **ko**-chay no a-**ran**-ka*

Do you have an emergency fan belt?
Tiene una correa de ventilador de emergencia?
*tee-**e**-nay **oo**-na ko-**ray**-a day ben-tee-la-**dor** day
  e-mair-**hen**-thee-a*

Do you have jump leads?
¿Tiene cables puente de batería?
*tee-**e**-nay **ka**-bles **pwen**-tay day ba-te-**ree**-a*

Do you have the spare parts?
¿Tiene los repuestos?
*tee-**e**-nay los re-**pwe**-stos*

Breakdowns and repairs

I have a flat tyre
Tengo un pinchazo
*ten-go oon peen-**cha**-tho*

I have blown a fuse
Se me ha quemado un fusible
*say may a ke-**ma**-do oon foo-**see**-blay*

I have locked myself out of the car
He cerrado el coche con las llaves dentro
*ay the-**ra**-do el **ko**-chay kon las **ya**-bes **den**-tro*

I have locked the ignition key inside the car
He dejado la llave de contacto dentro del coche
*ay de-**ha**-do la **ya**-bay day kon-**tak**-to **den**-tro del **ko**-chay*

I have run out of petrol
Me he quedado sin gasolina
*may ay ke-**da**-do seen ga-so-**lee**-na*

I need a new fan belt
Necesito una nueva correa de ventilador
*ne-the-**see**-to **oo**-na **nway**-ba ko-**ray**-a day ben-tee-la-**dor***

I think there is a bad connection
Creo que hay una mala conexión
kray**-o kay eye **oo**-na **ma**-la ko-nek-**syon

Is there a mechanic here?
¿Hay algún mecánico aquí?
*eye al-**goon** me-**ka**-nee-ko **a**-kee*

Breakdowns and repairs

The engine has broken down
Se ha averiado el motor
say a a-be-ree-a-do el mo-tor

There is something wrong
Hay algún problema
eye al-goon pro-blay-ma

There is something wrong with the car
Algo va mal en el coche
al-go ba mal en el ko-chay

Will it take long to repair it?
¿Tardará mucho en repararlo?
tar-da-ra moo-cho en re-pa-rar-lo

Is it serious?
¿Es grave?
es gra-bay

My windscreen has cracked
Se me ha rajado el parabrisas
say may a ra-ha-do el pa-ra-bree-sas

The air-conditioning does not work
No funciona el aire acondicionado
no foon-thyo-na el a-ee-ray a-kon-dee-thyo-na-do

The battery is flat
La batería está descargada
la ba-te-ree-a es-ta des-kar-ga-da

The engine is overheating
El motor se recalienta
el mo-tor say re-ka-lyen-ta

The exhaust pipe has fallen off
Se ha caído el tubo de escape
say a ka-ee-do el too-bo day es-ka-pay

There is a leak in the radiator
Hay una fuga en el radiador
eye oo-na foo-ga en el ra-dee-a-dor

Accidents and the police

Spain has three police forces. The Guardia Civil, who wear green uniforms, deal with law enforcement on the roads and in rural areas. The Policía Local, who wear blue and white uniforms, patrol within towns and can be approached about any difficulties. The Policía Nacional, who wear blue uniforms, guard public buildings and in all substantial towns man the *comisaría* (police station), where crimes may be reported. In addition, the autonomous communities of the Basque country, Catalonia, Galicia and Valencia have their own police forces. Telephone 091 for the Policía Nacional, 092 for the Policía Local.

There has been an accident
Ha habido un accidente
a a-bee-do oon ak-thee-den-tay

Accidents and the police

We must call an ambulance
Tenemos que llamar a una ambulancia
*te-**nay**-mos kay ya-**mar** a **oo**-na am-boo-**lan**-thee-a*

We must call the police
Tenemos que llamar a la policía
*te-**nay**-mos kay ya-**mar** a la po-lee-**thee**-a*

What is your name and address?
¿Cuál es su nombre y dirección?
*kwal es soo **nom**-bray ee dee-rek-**thyon***

You must not move
No debe moverse
*no **de**-bay mo-**bair**-say*

Do you want my passport?
¿Quiere mi pasaporte?
*kee-**e**-ray mee pa-sa-**por**-tay*

He did not stop
Él no paró
*el no pa-**ro***

He is a witness
Éste es testigo
*es-tay es te-**stee**-go*

He overtook on a bend
Él adelantó en una curva
*el a-de-lan-**to** en la **coor**-ba*

Accidents and the police

He ran into the back of my car
Él chocó con la parte trasera de mi coche
el cho-ko kon la par-tay tra-sair-a day mee ko-chay

He stopped suddenly
Él se paró de repente
el say pa-ro day re-pen-tay

He was moving too fast
Él iba demasiado rápido
el ee-ba de-ma-sya-a-do ra-pee-do

Here are my insurance documents
Aquí está la documentación del seguro
a-kee es-ta la do-koo-men-ta-thyon del se-goo-ro

Here is my driving licence
Aquí está mi permiso de conducir
a-kee es-ta mee pair-mee-so day kon-doo-theer

I could not stop in time
No he podido parar a tiempo
no ay po-dee-do pa-rar a tee-em-po

I did not see the bicycle
No vi la bicicleta
no bee la bee-thee-klay-ta

I did not see the sign
No vi la señal
no bee la sen-yal

Accidents and the police

I did not understand the sign
No entendí la señal
*no en-ten-**dee** la sen-**yal***

I am very sorry. I am a visitor
Lo siento mucho. Soy turista
*lo **syen**-to **moo**-cho. Soy too-**ree**-sta*

I did not know about the speed limit
No sabía lo del límite de velocidad
*no sa-**bee**-a lo del **lee**-mee-tay day be-lo-thee-**dad***

How much is the fine?
¿Cuánto es la multa?
***kwan**-to es la **mool**-ta*

I have not got enough money. Can I pay at the police station?
No tengo suficiente dinero ¿Puedo pagar en la comisaría de policía?
*no **ten**-go soo-fee-thee-**en**-tay dee-**ne**-ro. **Pwe**-do pa-gar en la ko-mee-sa-**ree**-a day po-lee-**thee**-a*

I have not had anything to drink
No he bebido nada
*no ay be-**bee**-do **na**-da*

I was only driving at 50 km/h
Sólo iba a cincuenta por hora
*so-lo **ee**-ba a theen-**kwen**-ta por **o**-ra*

Accidents and the police

I was overtaking
Estaba adelantando
*es-**ta**-ba a-de-lan-**tan**-do*

I was parking
Estaba aparcando
*es-**ta**-ba a-par-**kan**-do*

My car has been towed away
La grúa se ha llevado mi coche
*la **groo**-a say a ye-**ba**-do mee **ko**-chay*

That car was too close
Ese coche venía demasiado cerca
*e-say **ko**-chay be-**nee**-a de-ma-**sya**-do **thair**-ka*

The brakes failed
Los frenos fallaron
*los **fray**-nos fa-**ya**-ron*

The car number (license number) was...
La matrícula del coche era...
*la ma-**tree**-koo-la del **ko**-chay **ay**-ra...*

The car skidded
El coche derrapó
*el **ko**-chay de-ra-**po***

The car swerved
El coche giró bruscamente
*el **ko**-chay hee-**ro** broo-ska-**men**-tay*

Car parts

The car turned right without signalling
El coche giró a la derecha sin señalizar
*el **ko**-chay hee-**ro** a la de-**ray**-cha seen sen-ya-lee-**thar***

The road was icy
La carretera estaba congelada
*la ka-re-**tair**-a es-**ta**-ba kon-he-**la**-da*

The tyre burst
El neumático reventó
*el nay-oo-**ma**-tee-ko re-ben-**to***

Car parts

accelerator
acelerador
*a-the-le-ra-**dor***

aerial
antena
*an-**tay**-na*

air filter
filtro de aire
***feel**-tro day **eye**-ray*

alternator
alternador
*al-tair-na-**dor***

antifreeze
anticongelante
*an-tee-kon-he-**lan**-tay*

axle
eje
e-hay

battery
batería
*ba-te-**ree**-a*

bonnet
capó
*ka-**po***

boot
maletero
*ma-le-**te**-ro*

brake fluid
líquido de frenos
*lee-kee-do day **fray**-nos*

brakes
frenos
***fray**-nos*

bulb
foco
fo-ko

bumper
parachoques
*pa-ra-**cho**-kes*

car phone
teléfono de automóvil
*te-**le**-fo-no day ow-to-**mo**-beel*

carburettor
carburador
*kar-boo-ra-**dor***

child seat
silla de niño
***see**-ya day **neen**-yo*

choke
estárter
*e-**star**-tair*

clutch
embrague
*em-**bra**-gay*

cylinder
cilindro
*thee-**leen**-dro*

disc brake
freno de disco
***fray**-no day **dee**-sko*

distributor
distribuidor
*dees-tree-boo-ee-**dor***

door
portezuela
*por-tay-**thway**-la*

dynamo
dinamo
*dee-**na**-mo*

electrical system
sistema eléctrico
*see-**stay**-ma e-**lek**-tree-ko*

Car parts

engine
motor
mo-tor

exhaust system
sistema de escape
see-stay-ma day e-ska-pay

fan belt
correa del ventilador
ko-ray-a del ben-tee-la-dor

foot pump
bomba de pie
bom-ba day pee-ay

fuse
fusible
foo-see-blay

fuel pump
bomba de carburante
bom-ba day kar-boo-ran-tay

fuel gauge
indicador de carburante
een-dee-ka-dor day kar-boo-ran-tay

gear box
caja de cambios
ka-ha day kam-bee-os

gear lever
palanca de cambios
pa-lan-ka day kam-bee-os

generator
generador
he-ne-ra-dor

hammer
martillo
mar-tee-yo

hand brake
freno de mano
fray-no day ma-no

hazard lights
luces de emergencia
loo-thes day e-mair-hen-thee-a

headlights
faros
fa-ros

hood
capó
ka-po

horn
bocina
bo-thee-na

108

hose
manga
man-ga

ignition
contacto
kon-tak-to

ignition key
llave de contacto
ya-bay day kon-tak-to

indicator
intermitente
een-tair-mee-ten-tay

jack
gato
ga-to

lights
luces
loo-thes

lock
cerradura
the-ra-doo-ra

oil
aceite
a-thay-ee-tay

oil filter
filtro de aceite
feel-tro day a-thay-ee-tay

oil pressure
presión de aceite
pre-syon day a-thay-ee-tay

petrol
gasolina
ga-so-lee-na

points
platinos
pla-tee-nos

pump
bomba
bom-ba

radiator
radiador
ra-dee-a-dor

rear-view mirror
espejo retrovisor
es-pe-ho re-tro-bee-sor

reflectors
reflectantes
re-flek-tan-tes

Car parts

reversing light
luz de marcha atrás
*looth day **mar**-cha a-**tras***

roof rack
baca
***ba**-ka*

screwdriver
destornillador
*des-tor-nee-ya-**dor***

seat
asiento
*a-**syen**-to*

seat belt
cinturón de seguridad
*then-too-**ron** day se-goo-ree-**dad***

shock absorber
amortiguador
*a-mor-tee-gwa-**dor***

silencer
silenciador
*see-len-thee-a-**dor***

socket set
juego de llaves de tubo
***hway**-go day **ya**-bes day **too**-bo*

spanner
llave inglesa
*ya-bay een-**glay**-sa*

spare part
repuesto
*re-**pwe**-sto*

spark plug
bujía
*boo-**hee**-a*

speedometer
velocímetro
*be-lo-**thee**-me-tro*

starter motor
motor de arranque
*mo-**tor** day a-**ran**-kay*

steering
dirección
*dee-rek-**thyon***

steering wheel
volante
*bo-**lan**-tay*

stoplight
luz de freno
*looth day **fray**-no*

sun roof
techo solar
te-cho so-lar

suspension
suspensión
soo-spen-syon

tools
herramientas
e-ra-myen-tas

towbar
barra de remolque
ba-ra day re-mol-kay

transmission
transmisión
trans-mee-syon

trunk
maletero
ma-le-te-ro

tyre
neumático
nay-oo-ma-tee-ko

warning light
luz de advertencia
looth day ad-bair-ten-thee-a

wheel
rueda
roo-ay-da

windscreen
parabrisas
pa-ra-bree-sas

windscreen wipers
limpiaparabrisas
leem-pya-pa-ra-bree-sas

wrench
llave inglesa
ya-bay een-glay-sa

Road signs

Alto
al-to
Stop

111

Road signs

Aparcamiento sólo para residentes
a-par-ka-myen-to so-lo pa-ra re-see-den-tes
Parking for residents only

Camino particular
ka-mee-no par-tee-koo-lar
Private road

Ceda el paso
thay-da el pa-so
Give way

Centro ciudad
then-tro thee-oo-dad
Town centre

Circule por la derecha
theer-koo-lay por la de-ray-cha
Keep to the right

Deslizamientos
des-lee-tha-myen-tos
Icy roads

Despacio
des-pa-thee-o
Drive slowly

Desviación
des-bee-a-thyon
Diversion

Road signs

Desvío
des-bee-o
Diversion

Dirección única
dee-rek-thyon oo-nee-ka
One way

Estacionamiento de automóviles
es-ta-thyo-na-myen-to day ow-to-mo-bee-lays
Car park

Estacionamiento prohibido
es-ta-thyo-na-myen-to pro-ee-bee-do
No parking permitted

Obras
o-bras
Roadworks

Paso prohibido
pa-so pro-ee-bee-do
No through road

Peaje
pay-a-hay
Toll

Peligro
pay-lee-gro
Danger

113

Road signs

Prohibido el paso
*pro-ee-**bee**-do el **pa**-so*
No thoroughfare

No entrar
*no en-**trar***
No entry

EATING OUT

Dining in Spain is as much a reason for a social gathering as it is a matter of satisfying bodily needs or gastronomic indulgence. It is not something to be hurried. Despite the bustle of waiters scurrying around, you will rarely feel rushed in a restaurant – indeed, it is often an effort to extract the bill. Note, however, that in the big coastal resorts hotel meals are normally served buffet-style with international menus often presented in pictures.

There is a variety of options for eating out, but the uniquely Spanish one is the *tapas* bar. *Tapas* are small, savoury dishes of practically anything tasty – fish, squid, meats, olives, cheeses, vegetables, and so on. Select one or two small portions (*porciones*) for a snack or a selection of bigger portions (*raciones*) to make up a meal. The bars specialising in *tapas* are usually modest places, although some in the cities are beautifully tiled. You may eat your chosen delicacies at the bar over a beer or at a table (perhaps outside in a tourist area). *Tapas* are also served wherever snacks are likely to be in demand – in hotels, *bodegas* (wine cellars) *tabernas* (bars) or *tascas* (inns).

Away from the main resorts, main meal times are later than in most other countries. Lunch is the main meal of the day, mostly taken from about 2.00pm and often preceded by tapas. Restaurants open for lunch usually from 12.30 or

Reservations

1.00pm until 3.30 or 4.00pm. They re-open from about 7.30pm but do not do much business before 9.00pm. In cities, they will still be receiving diners at midnight.

In restaurants you will normally be encouraged to order *à la carte*, although there should also be a fixed menu of the day available. Menus are often broken down into kinds of dish – meat, fish, eggs, for example – rather than into courses.

Reservations

Should we reserve a table?
¿Deberíamos reservar mesa?
*de-be-**ree**-a-mos re-sair-**bar** may-sa*

Can I book a table for four at 8 o'clock?
¿Podría reservar una mesa para cuatro para las ocho?
*po-**dree**-a re-sair-**bar** oo-na **may**-sa **pa**-ra **kwa**-tro **pa**-ra las o-cho*

Can we have a table for four?
Una mesa para cuatro, por favor
oo**-na **may**-sa **pa**-ra **kwa**-tro, por fa-**bor

I am a vegetarian
Soy vegetariano / vegeteriana
*soy be-he-ta-ree-**a**-no / be-he-ta-ree-**a**-na)*

We would like a table — by the window
Nos gustaría una mesa — junto a la ventana
*nos goo-sta-**ree**-a **oo**-na **may**-sa* — ***hoon**-to a la ben-**ta**-na*

— on the terrace
— en la terraza
— *en la te-**ra**-tha*

Useful questions

Are vegetables included?
¿Se incluye verdura?
*say een-**kloo**-yay bair-**doo**-ra*

Do you have a local speciality?
¿Tienen alguna especialidad local?
*tee-**e**-nen al-**goo**-na es-peth-ya-lee-**dad** lo-**kal***

Do you have a set menu?
¿Tiene un menú del día?
*tee-**e**-nay oon me-**noo** del **dee**-a*

What do you recommend?
¿Qué me recomienda?
*kay may re-ko-**myen**-da*

What is the dish of the day?
¿Cuál es el plato del día?
*kwal es el **pla**-to del **dee**-a*

Useful questions

What is the soup of the day?
¿Cuál es la sopa del día?
kwal es la so-pa del dee-a

What is this called?
¿Cómo se llama esto?
ko-mo say ya-ma es-to

What is this dish like?
¿Cómo es este plato?
ko-mo es es-tay pla-to

Which local wine do you recommend?
¿Qué vino local recomienda?
kay bee-no lo-kal re-ko-myen-da

Do you have fruit?
¿Tiene fruta?
tee-e-nay froo-ta

How do I eat this?
¿Cómo se come esto?
ko-mo say ko-may es-to

Is the local wine good?
¿Es bueno el vino local?
es bway-no el bee-no lo-kal

Is this cheese very strong?
¿Es muy fuerte este queso?
es mwee fwair-tay es-tay ke-so

Is this good?
¿Está bueno esto?
es-ta bway-no es-to

What is this?
¿Qué es esto?
kay es es-to

Ordering your meal

The menu, please
El menú, por favor
el me-noo, por fa-bor

I will take the set menu
Tomaré el menú del día
to-ma-ray el me-noo del dee-a

Can we start with soup?
¿Podemos empezar con sopa?
po-day-mos em-pe-thar kon so-pa

I like my steak — very rare
    Me gusta — muy poco hecho
  may goo-sta — mwee po-ko e-cho

        — rare
        — poco hecho
      — po-ko e-cho

Ordering your meal

— **medium rare**
— medianamente hecho
— *me-dee-a-na-men-tay e-cho*

— **well done**
— bien hecho
— *bee-en e-cho*

Could we have some butter?
¿Puede traernos mantequilla, por favor?
pwe-day try-air-nos man-te-kee-ya, por fa-bor

We need some bread, please
Nos hace falta pan, por favor
nos a-thay fal-ta pan, por fa-bor

I will have salad
Yo tomaré ensalada
yo to-ma-ray en-sa-la-da

I will take that
Tomaré eso
to-ma-ray e-so

That is for me
Eso es para mí
e-so es pa-ra mee

Could we have some more bread please?
¿Puede traernos más pan por favor?
pwe-day try-air-nos mas pan, por fa-bor

Ordering drinks

Can I see the menu again, please?
¿Puedo volver a ver el menú, por favor?
*pwe-do bol-**bair** a bair el me-**noo**, por fa-**bor***

Ordering drinks

The wine list, please
La lista de vinos, por favor
*la **lee**-sta day **bee**-nos, por fa-**bor***

We will take the Rioja
Tomaremos el Rioja
*to-ma-**ray**-mos el ree-o-ha*

A bottle of house red wine, please
Una botella de vino tinto de la casa
*oo-na bo-**te**-ya day **bee**-no **teen**-to day la **ka**-sa*

A glass of dry white wine, please
Un vaso de vino blanco seco, por favor
*oon **ba**-so day **bee**-no **blan**-ko se-ko, por fa-**bor***

Another bottle of red wine, please
Otra botella de vino tinto, por favor
*o-tra bo-**te**-ya day **bee**-no **teen**-to, por fa-**bor***

Another glass, please
Otro vaso, por favor
*o-tro **ba**-so, por fa-**bor***

Paying the bill

Black coffee, please
Café solo, por favor
*ka-**fay** so-lo, por fa-**bor***

Can we have some (still / sparkling) mineral water?
¿Nos puede traer agua mineral (sin gas / con gas)?
*nos **pwe**-day try-**air** a-gwa mee-ne-**ral** (seen gas / con gas)*

Coffee with milk, please
Café con leche, por favor
*ka-**fay** kon **le**-chay, por fa-**bor***

Some plain water, please
Agua natural, por favor
a**-gwa na-too-**ral**, por fa-**bor

Two beers, please
Dos cervezas, por favor
*dos thair-**bay**-thas, por fa-**bor***

Paying the bill

Can we have the bill, please?
¿Puede traernos la cuenta, por favor?
pwe**-day try-**air**-nos la **kwen**-ta, por fa-**bor

Is service included?
¿Está el servicio incluido?
*es-**ta** el sair-**bee**-thee-o een-kloo-**ee**-do*

Complaints and compliments

Is tax included?
¿Están los impuestos incluidos?
*es-**tan** los eem-**pwe**-stos een-kloo-**ee**-dos*

Is there any extra charge?
¿Hay algún cargo adicional?
*a-ee al-**goon kar**-go a-deeth-yo-**nal***

I haven't enough money
No tengo suficiente dinero
*no **ten**-go soo-feeth-**yen**-tay dee-**ne**-ro*

This is not correct
Esto no es correcto
*es-to no es ko-**rek**-to*

This is not my bill
Ésta no es mi cuenta
*es-ta no es mee **kwen**-ta*

You have given me the wrong change
Me ha dado mal los cambios
*may a **da**-do mal los **kam**-bee-os*

Complaints and compliments

This is cold
Esto está frio
*es-to es-**ta free**-o*

Food

This is not what I ordered
Esto no es lo que he pedido
*es-to no es lo kay ay pe-**dee**-do*

Waiter! We have been waiting for a long time
¡Camarero! Estamos esperando desde hace mucho tiempo
*ka-ma-**rair**-o! Es-**ta**-mos es-pe-**ran**-do **dez**-day **a**-thay
moo-cho tee-**em**-po*

Can I have the recipe?
¿Puede darme la receta?
*pwe-day **dar**-may la re-**thay**-ta*

The meal was excellent
La comida estaba excelente
*la ko-**mee**-da es-**ta**-ba eks-the-**len**-tay*

This is excellent
Esto está buenísimo
*es-to es-**ta** bwe-**nee**-see-mo*

Food

Spanish food has an earthy richness, with pronounced flavours enhanced by different herbs and spices. There are some common factors across the country – the wide use of olive oil and garlic, for example – but also marked regional variations in the types of dishes and styles of cooking. There are relatively few national dishes, and only a handful have

Regional specialities

become internationally known – *tortilla* (omelette), *paella*, *gazpacho* and little else, but there is a good deal more to discover.

Stews (*cocidos*) and hotpots are the mainstay of much of the everyday Spanish diet, combining pulses such as rice or chickpeas with vegetables, meats, poultry and seafood, all enriched with peppers, herbs and spices. They make filling meals, particularly given the generous proportions of most Spanish servings – a feature of their hospitality.

But restaurant meals are much more sophisticated than this, at least in areas where there is the necessary affluent clientele. If food is your real passion, pack your brolly and head north to the Basque country, where gastronomy is alive and well.

The Spanish have a pronounced sweet tooth and have concocted many kinds of delicious sweet breads, pastries and sweetmeats, which they consume at every opportunity through the day, starting at breakfast with *churros* – sausage-shaped fritters – and *suizos* – sugar-topped sweet rolls.

Regional specialities

The Atlantic coast – the north coast, from Galicia across to the Basque country, has a mild, wet climate that ensures rich pastures for grazing and lots of fresh vegetables. The seafood too is about Spain's finest, and the cuisine reflects the quality of the produce used.

Regional specialities

Galicia has the greatest reputation for seafood, its ports supplying much of the rest of Spain. Octopus is a speciality, and the large prawns are irresistible. Galicians use either seafood or meats cooked with onions to fill their pies, called *empanadas*. Other dishes to look out for are *lacón con grelos*, a combination of salted ham, turnips and spicy *chorizo* sausages, and *caldo gallego*, which includes beans and cabbages in a meaty stew.

Asturias is famous for its *fabada* – so much so that it exports the rich meaty stew based on *fabes* (white beans). Fish is again a speciality, with excellent salmon and a fish stew known as *caldereta*. Try also the *merluza a la sidra*, hake cooked in cider.

The food of the **Basque country** is superb. Seafood and sauces are the Basques' forte, subtly combined in dishes such as cod cooked with peppers and onions – *bacalao a la vizcaína* – or cod in garlic and oil – *bacalao al pil-pil*. Also worth trying is sea bream – *besugo*. Some of the local specialities include baby eels – *anguilas* – which are fried in oil spiced with hot peppers and garlic. *Marmitako* (tuna stew) is also popular, as is the hake dish *kokotxas*.

South of the Pyrenees – meat replaces fish and seafood as the central element in the popular dishes of the regions south of the Pyrenees. The wine regions of Rioja and Navarra both have individual styles of cooking. Some of Rioja's most memorable dishes are those that involve cooking a variety of meats in red peppers and asparagus. Game is an important

Regional specialities

part of Navarra's cooking, drawing influences from both the Basques to the north and the Aragonese to the south. A popular home-grown dish of the region is trout cooked with ham – *trucha a la Navarra*.

Aragon – meats are the staple diet of the Aragonese, usually served with a rich red-pepper sauce called *chilindrón*. Another tasty dish is *magras con tomate*, using fried ham and a tomato-based sauce.

Catalonia's distinctive dishes have benefited from its position on the French border, laying it open to both French and Italian influences. Sauces are part of the attraction. Look out for *ali-oli*, made from olive oil and garlic beaten into a paste, and *picada*, made from almonds, pine nuts, garlic and parsley. Seafood is important. This is one of the best areas to try *zarzuela de mariscos* – mixed seafood stew – and Tarragona is noted for *romesco*, a distinctive sweetish sauce served with fish.

A simple, satisfying dish is *pan con tomate* – bread smeared with tomato and olive oil. As elsewhere in Spain, spicy sausages play an important part in the diet. Try *butifarra*, especially when served with *mangetes* (white beans). On the coast, you should try the mixture of chicken and lobster, and in Barcelona seek out the filling local *cocido* called *escudella* – it includes meat balls, a range of meats, pulses, vegetables and spices. Farther south, rice dishes are popular – *arroz a banda* is just rice cooked in a fish broth, which can be superb.

Regional specialities

Catalonians are keen on cakes. Among the sweet delicacies are *torteles* (*tortells* in Catalan) – filled rings of sweet bread – and *buñuelos* – fried puffs.

The southern Costas – paella originates from Valencia, and you should find some excellent examples in its home territory. As in the rest of Spain, *cocidos* are a major part of the everyday diet. Some to look out for are *cocido de pelotas* – meat in cabbage, chickpeas and potatoes – and *arroz con costra*, which includes chicken, rabbit, black pudding and more chickpeas.

Murcia is also strong on rice dishes. Try the fish one, *arroz al caldero*. Look out also for *menestra*, a vegetable stew. And for fish, try *mújol* (mullet), especially the roe.

Jijona is famous for its *túrron* – hard or soft nougat.

Andalucia is less distinguished in its cooking than some other regions, but it nevertheless gave birth to Spain's most famous soup, *gazpacho*. Fried fish – *pescaíto frito* – is a popular part of the diet, and from the land of flamenco comes *huevos a la flamenca* – eggs, ham, tomato, asparagus, *chorizo* and peppers.

Sweet specialities include *polvorones* – shortbread cookies – and *mostachones* – almond buns.

The meseta – in the central plateau regions, roast meats such as suckling pigs are popular. So are *cocidos* with lots of pulses, particularly chickpeas. Despite being landlocked, the central region still manages to produce some notable seafood dishes, drawing on the bountiful seas off Galicia. *Bacalao al* *ajo arriero* is one – cod cooked in garlic. Soups too are popular. Try some of the *sopas castellanas*, usually a type of meat broth.

If you like pork, ham or sausages, head for **Extremadura**. *Chorizos* take on myriad forms here, and the *Montánchez* ham is famous all over Spain. *Cocidos* are slightly less popular than in other regions. *Migas* is a tasty fried mixture of soaked bread, bacon and peppers.

A favourite sweet delicacy from **Ávila** is *yemas de Sta Teresa* – sugared egg yolks.

The Canary Islands – two of the most popular local dishes on the Canaries are again stews – *gofio* and *puchero canario*. Many dishes will be accompanied by the dressing known as *el mojo*, made of oil, vinegar, spices and garlic. The Canaries are one of the best places to sample *mazapanes* – marzipan cakes.

On the **Balearic Islands**, apart from an abundance of seafood, there are several meat dishes to try. *Sobrasada*, a peppery pork sausage, is one of the most common. On Majorca, try the enormous puff pastries, *ensaimadas*, and the sweet flans, *cocas*.

Menu reader

aceite
*a-**thay**-tay*
oil

aceitunas
*a-thay-**too**-nas*
olives

Menu reader

acelga
a-thel-ga
chard

aguacate
a-gwa-ka-tay
avocado

ajo
a-ho
garlic

albahaca
al-ba-a-ka
basil

albaricoques
al-ba-ree-ko-kes
apricots

albondigas
al-bon-dee-gas
meatballs

alcachofa
al-ka-cho-fa
artichoke

almejas
al-may-has
clams

apio
a-pee-o
celery

arroz con leche
a-roth kon le-chay
rice pudding

asado / asada la parrilla
a-sa-do / a-sa-da la pa-ree-ya
grilled

atún
a-toon
tuna

berenjena
be-ren-hay-na
aubergine

berro
be-ro
watercress

berza
ber-tha
cabbage

bizcocho
beeth-ko-cho
sponge cake

bocadillo
*bo-ka-**dee**-yo*
sandwich (with French-style
  bread)

bogavante a la marinera
*bo-ga-**ban**-tay a la
  ma-ree-**nair**-a*
lobster cooked in Galician
  style

bollos de pan
bo-yos day pan
bread rolls

budín
*boo-**deen***
pudding

buñuelos
*boon-yoo-**ay**-los*
doughnuts

caballa
*ka-**ba**-ya*
mackerel

caballa en escabeche
*ka-**ba**-ya en es-ka-**be**-chay*
marinated mackerel

cabezas de cordero al horno
*ka-**bay**-thas day kor-**dair**-o
  al **or**-no*
roast head of lamb (Aragon)

calabacín
*ka-la-ba-**theen***
courgette

calabaza
*ka-la-**ba**-tha*
squash

calamares
*ka-la-**ma**-res*
squid

caldo
kal-do
broth

caldo de pollo
*kal-do day **po**-yo*
chicken broth

caldo de vaca
*kal-do day **ba**-ka*
beef broth

callos
ka-yos
tripe

Menu reader

cangrejo de río
kan-gre-ho day ree-o
crayfish

carne
kar-nay
meat

carne asada
kar-nay a-sa-da
grilled meat

carne de vaca en asador
kar-nay day ba-ka en a-sa-dor
braised beef

castañas asadas
kas-tan-yas a-sa-das
roast chestnuts

cebollas
the-bo-yas
onions

cebollinos
the-bo-yee-nos
chives

cerdo asado
thair-do a-sa-do
pork roast

cerezas
the-ray-thas
cherries

chalotes
cha-lo-tes
shallots

champiñones
cham-peen-yo-nes
mushrooms

champiñones al ajillo
cham-peen-yo-nes al a-hee-yo
mushrooms with garlic

champiñones en salsa
cham-peen-yo-nes en sal-sa
mushrooms in sauce

chirivía
chee-ree-bee-a
parsnip

chorizo
cho-ree-tho
hard pork sausage

chuleta de cerdo
choo-lay-ta day thair-do
pork chop

chuleta de cordero
*choo-**lay**-ta day kor-**dair**-o*
lamb chop

chuleta de ternera
*choo-**lay**-ta day tair-**nair**-a*
veal cutlet

churros
***choo**-ros*
fritters

ciruelas
*thee-roo-**ay**-las*
plums

cochinillo asado
*ko-chee-**nee**-yo a-**sa**-do*
roast suckling pig (Castile)

cocido de alubias
*ko-**thee**-do day a-**loo**-byas*
bean stew

cocido madrileño
*ko-**thee**-do ma-dree-**len**-yo*
meat stew with vegetables

coles de Bruselas
***ko**-les day broo-**say**-las*
Brussels sprouts

coliflor
*ko-lee-**flor***
cauliflower

compota de manzana
*kom-**po**-ta day man-**tha**-na*
apple compote

conejo con caracoles
*ko-**ne**-ho kon ka-ra-**ko**-les*
rabbit with snails

conejo estofado
*ko-**ne**-ho e-sto-**fa**-do*
stuffed rabbit

cordero en asador
*kor-**dair**-o en a-sa-**dor***
mutton on the spit

dátiles
***da**-tee-les*
dates

ensalada
*en-sa-**la**-da*
salad

ensalada de maíz
*en-sa-**la**-da day my-**eeth***
corn salad

133

Menu reader

ensalada de patata
*en-sa-**la**-da day pa-**ta**-ta*
potato salad

ensalada de pepino
*en-sa-**la**-da day pe-pee-**nee**-yo*
cucumber salad

ensalada de tomate
*en-sa-**la**-da day to-**ma**-tay*
tomato salad

ensalada mixta
*en-sa-**la**-da **meek**-sta*
mixed salad

ensaladilla rusa
*en-sa-la-**dee**-ya **roo**-sa*
Russian salad

. . . en salsa
*. . . en **sal**-sa*
. . . in sauce

escarola
*e-ska-**ro**-la*
chicory

espaguetis
*es-pa-**ge**-tees*
spaghetti

espárragos
*es-**pa**-ra-gos*
asparagus

espinacas
*es-pee-**na**-kas*
spinach

estragón
*es-tra-**gon***
tarragon

fabada
*fa-**ba**-da*
bean and pork stew (Asturias)

faisán
*fy-ee-**san***
pheasant

filete
*fee-**le**-tay*
fillet steak

filete de merluza
*fee-**le**-tay day mair-**loo**-tha*
hake fillet

filete de vaca
*fee-**le**-tay day **ba**-ka*
beefsteak

flan
flan
crème caramel

frambuesas
fram-bway-sas
raspberries

fresas
fray-sas
strawberries

fresas con nata
fray-sas kon na-ta
strawberries and cream

fruta con nata montada
froo-ta kon na-ta mon-ta-da
fruit with whipped cream

gazpacho
gath-pa-cho
cold soup with cucumber,
  tomato, garlic etc

granada
gra-na-da
pomegranate

grosellas negras
gro-se-yas ne-gras
blackcurrants

guisado de carne
gee-sa-do day kar-nay
beef stew

guisado de pollo
gee-sa-do day po-yo
chicken stew

guisantes
gee-san-tes
peas

habas
a-bas
broad beans

helado
e-la-do
ice cream

hierbabuena
yair-ba-bway-na
mint

hoja de laurel
o-ha day low-rel
bayleaf

huevo pasado por agua
way-bo pa-sa-do por a-gwa
soft boiled egg

Menu reader

huevos con jamón
way-bos kon ha-mon
eggs with ham

huevos con tocino
way-bos kon to-thee-no
eggs with bacon

huevos fritos
way-bos free-tos
fried eggs

huevos revueltos
way-bos re-bwel-tos
scrambled eggs

jamón serrano
ha-mon se-ra-no
cured ham

judías verdes
hoo-dee-as bair-des
French beans

langosta
lan-go-sta
lobster

langostinos rebozados
lan-go-stee-nos re-bo-tha-dos
scampi

lechón en asador
le-chon en a-sa-dor
suckling pig on the spit

lechuga
le-choo-ga
lettuce

lengua
len-gwa
tongue

limón
lee-mon
lemon

macedonia de frutas
ma-the-do-nee-a day froo-tas
fruit salad

maíz
my-eeth
sweet corn

mantequilla
man-te-kee-ya
butter

manzana asada
man-tha-na a-sa-da
roast apple

manzanas
man-tha-nas
apples

mejillones
me-hee-yo-nes
mussels

melocotón
me-lo-ko-ton
peach

melón
me-lon
melon

merluza en salsa verde
*mair-loo-tha en sal-sa
bair-day*
hake in parsley sauce

mermelada
mair-me-la-da
jam

morcilla
mor-thee-ya
black pudding (= blood
sausage)

mousse de chocolate
moos day cho-ko-la-tay
chocolate mousse

nabo
na-bo
turnip

naranjas
na-ran-has
oranges

natillas
na-tee-yas
custard

oca
o-ka
goose

ostras
o-stras
oysters

ostras fritas
o-stras free-tas
fried oysters (Galicia)

paella
py-e-ya
paella

137

Menu reader

pasta
pa-sta
pasta

patas de rana fritas
pa-tas day ra-na free-tas
fried frog legs

patatas a la riojana
pa-ta-tas a la ree-o-ha-na
potatoes cooked with
tomatoes and haricot beans
(Rioja)

patatas asadas
pa-ta-tas a-sa-das
roast potatoes

patatas bravas
pa-ta-tas bra-bas
spicy fried potatoes

patatas fritas
pa-ta-tas free-tas
French fries

**patatas troceadas y
verdura con mayonesa**
*pa-ta-tas tro-thay-a-das y
bair-doo-ra kon my-o nay-sa*
cubed potatoes and vegetables
with mayonnaise

pato
pa-to
duck

pato relleno con manzanas
*pa-to re-yay-no kon
man-tha-nas*
roast duck with apples

pavo
pa-bo
turkey

pepinillo
pe-pee-nee-yo
gherkin

pepino
pe-pee-no
cucumber

pera
pay-ra
pear

perdiz en chocolate
pair-deeth en cho-ko-la-tay
partridge with a chocolate
sauce (Navarra)

perejil
pe-re-heel
parsley

perifollo
pe-ree-fo-yo
chervil

perrito caliente
pe-ree-to kal-lee-en-tay
hot dog

pescado
pes-ka-do
fish

pescado en escabeche
pes-ka-do en es-ka-be-chay
marinated fish

pierna (de cordero, etc)
pee-air-na (day kor-dair-o, etc)
shank (of lamb, etc)

pimiento rojo
pee-myen-to ro-ho
red pepper

pimiento verde
pee-myen-to bair-day
green pepper

pimientos rellenos
pee-myen-tos re-yay-nos
stuffed peppers

piña
peen-ya
pineapple

plátano
pla-ta-no
banana

pollo cocido / asado
po-yo ko-thee-do / a-sa-do
baked / roasted chicken

pollo frito/rebozado
po-yo free-to/re-bo-tha-do
fried/breaded chicken

pomelo
po-me-lo
grapefruit

puerros
pwe-ros
leeks

puré de patatas
poo-ray day pa-ta-tas
mashed potatoes

queso
ke-so
cheese

queso manchego
ke-so man-chay-go
la Mancha cheese

rábanos
ra-ba-nos
radishes

remolacha
re-mo-la-cha
beetroot

riñones guisados
reen-yo-nes gee-sa-dos
stewed kidney

romero
ro-mair-o
rosemary

salchicha
sal-chee-cha
sausage

salmonete
sal-mo-ne-tay
mullet

salsa de cebolla
sal-sa day the-bo-ya
onion sauce

salsa de manzana
sal-sa day man-tha-na
applesauce

salsa de pimiento verde
sal-sa day pee-myen-to
green pepper sauce

salsa de tomate
sal-sa day to-ma-tay
tomato sauce

salsa de vino
sal-sa day bee-no
wine sauce

salvia
sal-bee-a
sage

sandía
san-dee-a
watermelon

sandwich de jamón
san-weech day ha-mon
ham sandwich

sardinas
sar-dee-nas
sardines

sepia
se-pee-a
cuttlefish

sopa de ajo
so-pa day a-ho
garlic soup

sopa de crema de
 champiñones
*so-pa day kray-ma day
 cham-peen-yo-nes*
cream of mushroom soup

sopa de fideos
so-pa day fee-day-os
noodle soup

sopa de frijoles
so-pa day free-ho-les
kidney-bean soup

sopa de guisantes
so-pa day gee-san-tes
pea soup

sopa de pollo
so-pa day po-yo
chicken soup

sopa de puerros
so-pa day pwe-ros
leek soup

sopa de tomate
so-pa day to-ma-tay
tomato soup

tallarines de huevo
ta-ya-ree-nes day way-bo
egg noodles

tarta
tar-ta
cake/pie

tarta de almendra
tar-ta day al-men-dra
almond cake

tarta de limón
tar-ta day lee-mon
lemon meringue

tarta de manzana
tar-ta day man-tha-na
apple cake

tomates
to-ma-tes
tomatoes

tomillo
to-mee-yo
thyme

Wine

tortas
tor-tas
thin pancakes

— con chocolate
— kon cho-ko-la-tay
—with chocolate

— con mermelada
— kon mair-me-la-da
—with jam

tortilla española
tor-tee-ya es-pan-yo-la
Spanish omelette

trucha
troo-cha
trout

trucha cocida
troo-cha ko-thee-da
boiled trout

trucha frita
troo-cha free-ta
fried trout

uvas
oo-bas
grapes

verduras
bair-doo-ras
vegetables

vinagre
bee-na-gray
vinegar

yogur
yo-goor
yoghurt

zanahoria
tha-na-o-ree-a
carrot

Wine

As in France and Italy, there is a system of specified wine names in Spain, which may be applied only to wines produced from particular areas, in particular ways, using particular grapes. The Spanish system does not attempt to pin

Wine regions

down the geographical origin with any precision. The area covered by a single Denominación de Origen (DO) may be enormous. There are only thirty demarcated regions, compared with over three hundred in France. The regulations are also somewhat general. The result is that DO status does not mean a great deal and that the reputation of individual producers is the key to identifying good wine.

Since joining the European Union, Spain has gained another wine classification – vinos de la tierra – along the lines of the French vins de pays system. The regulations specify grape varieties (up to a point) and minimum alcohol levels.

Spanish winemaking has improved a lot in recent years, but the biggest revolution has been in white winemaking. Most exported whites are now made fresh and fruity, if rather neutral in flavour, taking after the main white grapes, the Airén and the Viura. Reds from the Penedés and Rioja can be extremely good.

Wine regions
Catalonia – the most important wines of Catalonia in the northeast are from Penedés, the area inland from the coast south of Barcelona. The reds – particularly those based on the non-native Cabernet Sauvignon – rival the wines of Rioja, but the area is also the major producer of Cava – Spain's sparking wines fermented by the Champagne method. The areas southwest of Penedés (Priorato, Tarragona, Terra Alta) produce some weighty reds.

Wine regions

Navarra – west of Catalonia – shares the northern flank of the Ebro valley with Rioja but until recently did not achieve the quality or status of its neighbour. Now there are excellent reds to be had – both light wine for drinking young and heavier, barrel-aged ones. Recent white vintages are satisfactorily zippy.

Rioja is easily the best known of Spain's wine regions. South of Navarra, it is divided into three areas straddling the River Ebro. It is from Rioja Alta and Rioja Alavesa (scenic, hilly, upstream areas, north and south of the river) that the best of the wines originate. The flat, hot Rioja Baja produces heavier wines often used to bolster the more delicate reds from upstream. The maturing of wines, especially the reds, in oak casks is the region's distinctive feature, giving a pronounced vanilla flavour.

Galicia – in the northwest, this area's proximity to Portugal's *vinho verde* country is reflected in its sharp white wines.

Ribera del Duero – north of Madrid, this medium-sized DO area – 'the banks of the Duero' – is realising its potential for the production of fine reds.

Rueda – this region north of Madrid is traditionally known for sherry-style wines made from the Palamino grape but it now produces mainly fresh, nutty white table wines from the native Verdejo grape.

La Mancha and Valdepeñas – these two areas south of Madrid together form by far the largest wine-producing region

in the country, making some very agreeable reds and whites.
Although they may lack the subtleties of Riojas and Penedés,
there are some *reservas* and *gran reservas* worth attention.

Sherry – from in and around Jerez in the far south (or indeed
from Spain in general) – bears little relation to the sweetened
products sold in volume in Britain.

There are two basic varieties of sherry. *Fino* is pale and dry
with a pronounced tang that comes from a natural yeast (*flor*)
that forms on the surface of the wine in the barrel. Only light,
fresh, fine wines are susceptible. An *amontillado* starts out
as *fino* but is aged until the *flor* dies. Although deeper in colour, it is still dry. *Olorosos* are richer in colour but also dry,
made from heavier wines more heavily fortified, without the
formation of *flor*.

Wine label reader

abrocado
a-bro-ka-do
medium sweet

almacenista
al-ma-the-nee-sta
unblended sherry with distinctive flavours

amontillado
a-mon-tee-ya-do
aged *fino* – darker, deeper but still very dry

Wine label reader

blanco
blan-ko
white

bodega
bo-day-ga
wine cellar (wherever wine is made, stored or sold)

brut
broot
dry

cava
ka-ba
wine made by the Champagne method

clarete
kla-re-tay
light red

criado y embotellado por . . .
kree-a-do ee em-bo-te-ya-do por . . .
grown and bottled by . . .

(de) crianza
(day) kree-an-tha
aged in wood

dulce
dool-thay
sweet

embotellado de origen
em-bo-te-ya-do day o-*ree*-hen
estate-bottled

espumoso
es-poo-mo-so
sparkling wine

fino
fee-no
pale, very dry sherry made from the lightest wines, to be drunk cool and young

generoso
he-ne-ro-so
aperitif or dessert wine

gran reserva
gran re-sair-ba
top quality Rioja wine, aged for longer before sale than *reserva* but capable of further ageing. The meaning may be different for wines from outside Rioja

Other drinks

manzanilla
*man-tha-**nee**-ya*
form of fino

nuevo
***nway**-bo*
young wine

oloroso
*o-lo-**ro**-so*
dark sherry made from richer
  wines and more heavily
  fortified but still dry

reserva
*re-**sair**-ba*
selected Rioja wine from a
  good vintage, aged for a
  minimum period before
  sale, at which point it is
  generally ready to drink

rosado
*ro-**sa**-do*
rosé

seco
***say**-ko*
dry

semi-seco
*se-mee-**say**-ko*
medium dry

sin crianza
*seen **kree**-an-tha*
not aged in wood

tinto
***teen**-to*
red

Other drinks

agua mineral
***a**-gwa mee-**ne**-ral*
mineral water

aguardiente
*a-gwar-dee-**en**-tay*
brandy

Other drinks

aguardiente de cerezas
a-gwar-dee-en-tay day the-ray-thas
cherry brandy

aguardiente de manzanas
a-gwar-dee-en-tay day man-tha-nas
apple brandy

anís
a-nees
anis

café
ka-fay
coffee

café americano
ka-fay a-me-ree-ka-no
large black coffee

café con hielo
ka-fay kon ye-lo
iced coffee

café con leche
ka-fay kon le-chay
white coffee

café escocés
ka-fay es-ko-thes
coffee with whisky and ice cream

café instantáneo
ka-fay een-stan-ta-nay-o
instant coffee

café irlandés
ka-fay eer-lan-des
Irish coffee

café sólo
ka-fay so-lo
small black coffee

una caña
oo-na kan-ya
a small glass of draught beer

carajillo
ka-ra-hee-yo
coffee with a dash of brandy

capuchino
ka-poo-chee-no
cappuccino

cerveza
thair-bay-tha
beer

cerveza embotellada
*thair-**bay**-tha em-bo-te-**ya**-da*
bottled beer

cerveza enlatada
*thair-**bay**-tha en-la-**ta**-da*
canned beer

una cerveza grande
***oo**-na thair-**bay**-tha **gran**-day*
a large beer

cerveza negra
*thair-**bay**-tha **ne**-gra*
stout

champán
*cham-**pan***
champagne

coca-cola
*ko-ka-**ko**-la*
coke

un coñac
*oon kon-**yak***
a brandy

cortado
*kor-**ta**-do*
coffee with a dash of milk

descafeinado
*des-ka-fay-**na**-do*
decaffeinated coffee

horchata
*or-**cha**-ta*
tiger nut milk

licor
*lee-**kor***
liqueur

limonada
*lee-mo-**na**-da*
lemonade

manzanilla
*man-tha-**nee**-ya*
camomile tea

naranjada
*na-ran-**ha**-da*
orange drink

pacharán
*pa-cha-**ran***
a type of sloe gin

ron
ron
rum

149

Other drinks

sangría
san-gree-a
fruit cup with wine

sidra
see-dra
cider

soda
so-da
soda water

té
tay
tea

té con leche
tay kon le-chay
tea with milk

té con limón
tay kon lee-mon
lemon tea

tónica
to-nee-ka
tonic water

un vaso de vino blanco
oon ba-so day bee-no blan-ko
a glass of white wine

un vaso de vino tinto
oon ba-so day bee-no teen-to
a glass of red wine

vermut
bair-moot
vermouth

vino rosado
bee-no ro-sa-do
rosé wine

zumo de albaricoque
thoo-mo day al-ba-ree-ko-kay
apricot juice

zumo de manzana
thoo-mo day man-tha-na
apple juice

zumo de melocotón
thoo-mo day me-lo-ko-ton
peach juice

zumo de naranja
thoo-mo day na-ran-ha
orange juice

zumo de uva
thoo-mo day oo-ba
grape juice

OUT AND ABOUT

The weather

The northern coastal regions catch all the rain clouds coming off the Atlantic, making this area wet and often windy. Relatively little rain crosses the mountains to the elevated central plateau where the climate can be harsh, with blisteringly hot summer days and freezing winter nights. In winter, much of the Pyrenees may be snowbound. (There is skiing here and in the very high Sierra Nevada in the extreme south.) The Mediterranean coasts enjoy milder climates of hot dry summers and cool damp winters. The Canaries have reliably sunny summers and warm winters.

Is it going to get any warmer?
¿Va a hacer más calor?
*ba a a-**thair** mas ka-**lor***

Is it going to stay like this?
¿Va a continuar así?
*ba a kon-tee-**nwar** a-**see***

Is there going to be a thunderstorm?
¿Va a haber tormenta?
*ba a a-**bair** tor-**men**-ta*

The weather

Isn't it a lovely day?
¿No es éste un día maravilloso?
*no es **es**-tay oon **dee**-a ma-ra-bee-**yo**-so*

It has stopped snowing
Ha parado de nevar
*a pa-**ra**-do day ne-**bar***

It is a very clear night
Hace una noche muy despejada
*a-thay **oo**-na **no**-chay mwee des-pe-**ha**-da*

It is far too hot
Hace demasiado calor
*a-thay de-ma-**sya**-do ka-**lor***

It is foggy
Hay niebla
*eye nee-**e**-bla*

It is raining again
Está lloviendo de nuevo
*es-**ta** yo-**byen**-do day **nway**-bo*

It is very cold
Hace mucho frío
*a-thay **moo**-cho **free**-o*

It is very windy
Hace mucho viento
*a-thay **moo**-cho bee-**en**-to*

There is a cool breeze
Hay una brisa fresca
eye oo-na bree-sa fre-ska

What is the temperature?
¿Qué temperatura hace?
kay tem-pe-ra-too-ra a-thay

It is going — to be fine
Va — a hacer bueno
ba — a a-thair bway-no

— to be windy
— a hacer viento
— a a-thair bee-en-to

— to rain
— a llover
— a yo-bair

— to snow
— a nevar
— a ne-bar

Will it be cold tonight?
¿Hará frío esta noche?
a-ra free-o es-ta no-chay

Will the weather improve?
¿Va a mejorar el tiempo?
ba a me-ho-rar el tee-em-po

On the beach

Will the wind die down?
¿Va a amainar el viento?
*ba a a-my-**nar** el bee-**en**-to*

On the beach

Can we change here?
¿Podemos cambiarnos aquí?
*po-**day**-mos kam-**byar**-nos a-**kee***

Can you recommend a quiet beach?
¿Puede sugerir una playa tranquila?
*pwe-day soo-he-**reer oo**-na **ply**-a tran-**kee**-la*

Is it safe to swim here?
¿Es seguro nadar aquí?
*es se-**goo**-ro na-**dar** a-**kee***

Is the current strong?
¿Hay mucha corriente?
*eye **moo**-cha ko-ree-**en**-tay*

Is the sea calm?
¿Está la mar tranquila?
*es-**ta** la mar tran-**kee**-la*

Can I rent — a sailing boat?
¿Puedo alquilar — un barco de vela?
*pwe-do al-kee-**lar** — oon **bar**-ko day **bay**-la*

> **— a rowing boat?**
> — un bote de remos?
> — *oon **bo**-tay day **re**-mos*

Is it possible to go — sailing?
¿Es posible — salir a navegar?
*es po-**see**-blay — sa-**leer** a na-be-**gar***

> **— surfing?**
> — hacer surf?
> — *a-**thair** soorf*

> **— water skiing?**
> — hacer esquí acuático?
> — *a-**thair** e-**skee** a-**kwa**-tee-ko*

> **— wind surfing?**
> — hacer windsurf?
> — *a-**thair** **ween**-soorf*

Is the water warm?
¿Está el agua templada?
*es-**ta** el **a**-gwa tem-**pla**-da*

Is there a heated swimming pool?
¿Hay alguna piscina climatizada?
*eye al-**goo**-na pees-**thee**-na klee-ma-tee-**tha**-da*

Is there a lifeguard here?
¿Hay algún salvavidas aquí?
*eye al-**goon** sal-ba-**bee**-das a-**kee***

Sport and recreation

Is this beach private?
¿Es privada esta playa?
*es pree-**ba**-da **es**-ta **ply**-a*

When is high tide?
¿Cuándo toca marea alta?
***kwan**-do **to**-ka ma-**ray**-a **al**-ta*

When is low tide?
¿Cuándo toca marea baja?
***kwan**-do **to**-ka ma-**ray**-a **ba**-ha*

Sport and recreation

Can I rent the equipment?
¿Puedo alquilar el material?
pwe**-do al-kee-**lar** el ma-te-ree-**al

Can we go riding?
¿Podemos ir a montar a caballo?
*po-**day**-mos eer a mon-**tar** a ka-**ba**-yo*

   Can we — play tennis?
¿Podemos — jugar al tenis?
*po-**day**-mos — hoo-**gar** al **te**-nees*

      — play golf?
      — jugar al golf?
      *— hoo-**gar** al golf*

— **play volleyball?**
— jugar al voleibol?
— *hoo-**gar** al bo-lee-**bol***

Where can we fish?
¿Dónde podemos pescar?
don**-day po-**day**-mos pe-**skar

Do we need a permit?
¿Necesitamos permiso?
*ne-the-see-**ta**-mos pair-**mee**-so*

Entertainment

How much is it for a child?
¿Cuánto cuesta para un niño?
***kwan**-to kwe-sta **pa**-ra oon **neen**-yo*

How much is it per person?
¿Cuánto cuesta por persona?
***kwan**-to kwe-sta por pair-**so**-na*

How much is it to get in?
¿Cuánto cuesta la entrada?
***kwan**-to kwe-sta la en-**tra**-da*

 Is there — a disco?
  ¿Hay — alguna discoteca?
   *eye — al-**goo**-na dee-sko-**tay**-ka*

Sightseeing

> **— a good nightclub?**
> — algún buen club?
> — *al-**goon** bwen kloob*

> **— a theatre?**
> — teatro?
> — *tay-**a**-tro*

Are there any films in English?
¿Hay alguna película en inglés?
*eye al-**goo**-na pe-**lee**-koo-la en een-**gles***

Two stalls tickets, please
Dos entradas en butacas, por favor
*dos en-**tra**-das en boo-**ta**-kas, por fa-**bor***

Two tickets, please
Dos entradas, por favor
*dos en-**tra**-das, por fa-**bor***

Is there a reduction for children?
¿Hay descuento para niños?
*eye des-**kwen**-to **pa**-ra **neen**-yos*

Sightseeing

Are there any boat trips on the river?
¿Hay excursiones en barco por el río?
*eye ek-skoor-**syo**-nes en **bar**-ko por el **ree**-o*

Are there any guided tours of the castle?
¿Hay alguna visita con guía al castillo?
*eye al-**goo**-na bee-**see**-ta kon **gee**-a al ka-**stee**-yo*

Are there any guided tours?
¿Hay visitas con guía?
*eye bee-**see**-tas kon **gee**-a*

What is there to see here?
¿Qué hay para ver aquí?
*kay eye **pa**-ra bair a-**kee***

What is this building?
¿Qué es este edificio?
*kay es **es**-tay e-dee-**fee**-thee-o*

When was it built?
¿Cuándo se construyó?
kwan**-do say kon-stroo-**yo

Is it open to the public?
¿Está abierto al público?
*es-**ta** a-bee-**air**-to al **poo**-blee-ko*

What is the admission charge?
¿Cuánto cuesta la entrada?
***kwan**-to **kwes**-ta la en-**tra**-da*

Can we go in?
¿Podemos entrar?
*po-**day**-mos en-**trar***

Sightseeing

Can we go up to the top?
¿Podemos subir hasta arriba?
*po-**day**-mos soo-**beer** a-sta a-**ree**-ba*

Can I take photos?
¿Puedo hacer fotos?
***pwe**-do a-**thair** fo-tos*

Can I use flash?
¿Puedo utilizar flash?
***pwe**-do oo-tee-lee-**thar** flas*

How long does the tour take?
¿Cuánto dura la excursión?
kwan**-to **doo**-ra la ek-skoor-**syon

Is there a guide book?
¿Hay alguna guía turística?
*eye al-**goo**-na **gee**-a too-**ree**-stee-ka*

Is there a tour of the cathedral?
¿Hay visita a la catedral?
*eye bee-**see**-ta a la ka-te-**dral***

Is there an English-speaking guide?
¿Hay algún guía que hable inglés?
*eye al-**goon gee**-a kay **a**-blay een-**gles***

Is this the best view?
¿Es ésta la mejor vista?
*es **es**-ta la me-**hor bee**-sta*

What time does the gallery open?
¿A qué hora abre la galería?
a kay o-ra a-bray la ga-le-ree-a

When is the bus tour?
¿Cuándo es la visita en autobús?
kwan-do es la bee-see-ta en ow-to-boos

Souvenirs

Have you got an English guidebook?
¿Tiene alguna guía turística en inglés?
tee-e-nay al-goo-na gee-a too-ree-stee-ka en een-gles

Have you got any colour slides?
¿Tiene diapositivas en color?
tee-e-nay dee-a-po-zee-tee-bas en ko-lor

Where can I buy postcards?
¿Dónde puedo comprar postales?
don-day pwe-do kom-prar po-sta-les

Where can we buy souvenirs?
¿Dónde podemos comprar recuerdos?
don-day po-day-mos kom-prar re-kwair-dos

Going to church

When visiting a church, dress appropriately. Do not wear shorts or short skirts, and ensure that your shoulders are covered. If you are just sightseeing, it is advisable to arrange to visit when there is not a religious service in progress.

Where is the — **Catholic church?**
¿Dónde está la — iglesia Católica?
don-day es-ta la — *ee-glay-see-a ka-to-lee-ka*

— **Baptist church?**
— la iglesia Bautista?
— *la ee-glay-see-a bow-tee-sta*

— **mosque?**
— la mezquita?
— *la meth-kee-ta*

— **Protestant church?**
— iglesia Protestante?
— *ee-glay-see-a pro-te-stan-tay*

— **synagogue?**
— la sinagoga?
— *la see-na-go-ga*

What time is mass?
¿A qué hora es la misa?
a kay o-ra es la mee-sa

I would like to see — a priest
Me gustaría hablar con — un sacerdote
*may goo-sta-**ree**-a a-**blar** kon* — *oon sa-thair-**do**-tay*

— **a minister**
— un pastor
— *oon pa-**stor***

— **a rabbi**
— un rabino
— *oon ra-**bee**-no*

SHOPPING

Most shops in smaller towns tend to follow the traditional pattern of the siesta, closing from lunchtime until 4.00 or 4.30pm, then staying open until 7.00pm or later. In the cities and in the busy resorts, however, you will find many shops and department stores stay open all day. Most shops are closed on public holidays (*see* page 228).

General phrases and requests

How much does that cost?
¿Cuánto cuesta eso?
kwan-to kwes-ta e-so

How much is it — per kilo?
 ¿Cuánto cuesta — por kilo?
kwan-to kwes-ta— por kee-lo

                    — per metre?
                    — por metro?
                    — por me-tro

How much is this?
¿Cuánto es esto?
kwan-to es es-to

General phrases and requests

Have you got anything cheaper?
¿Tiene algo más barato?
*tee-e-nay **al**-go mas ba-**ra**-to*

Can I see that umbrella?
¿Puedo ver ese paraguas?
*pwe-do bair e-say pa-**ra**-gwas*

No, the other one
No, el otro
*no, el **o**-tro*

Can you deliver to my hotel?
¿Puede entregármelo al hotel?
*pwe-day en-tre-**gar**-may-lo al o-**tel***

I do not like it
No me gusta
*no may **goo**-sta*

I like this one
Me gusta éste
*may **goo**-sta **es**-tay*

I will take — this one
    Tomaré — éste
*to-ma-**ray** — **es**-tay*

    — that one
    — ése
    — e-say

General phrases and requests

> **— the other one**
> — el otro
> — *el o-tro*

> **— that one over there**
> — aquél de allí
> — *a-kel day a-ye*

Where can I buy some clothes?
¿Dónde puedo comprar ropa?
don-day pwe-do kom-prar ro-pa

Where can I buy tapes for my camcorder?
¿Dónde puedo comprar cintas para el camcórder?
don-day pwe-do kom-prar theen-tas pa-ra el kam-kor-dair

Where can I get my camcorder repaired?
¿A dónde puedo llevar a reparar el camcórder?
a don-day pwe-do ye-bar a re-pa-rar el kam-kor-dair

> **Where is — the children's department?**
> ¿Dónde está — el departamento infantil?
> *don-day es-ta — el de-par-ta-men-to een-fan-teel*

> **— the food department?**
> — el departamento de comestibles?
> — *el de-par-ta-men-to day ko-me-stee-blays*

I am looking for a souvenir
Estoy buscando un recuerdo
es-toy boo-skan-do oon re-kwair-do

General phrases and requests

Do you sell sunglasses?
¿Venden gafas de sol?
ben-den ga-fas day sol

    Can I have — a carrier bag?
  ¿Puede darme — una bolsa?
pwe-day dar-may— oo-na bol-sa

              — a receipt?
              — un recibo?
              — oon re-thee-bo

              — an itemised bill?
              — una cuenta detallada?
              — oo-na kwen-ta de-ta-ya-da

Can I pay for air insurance?
¿Puedo pagar un seguro aéreo?
pwe-do pa-gar oon se-goo-ro a-air-ay-o

What is the total?
¿Cuánto es el total?
kwan-to es el to-tal

Do you accept traveller's cheques?
¿Acepta cheques de viaje?
a-thep-ta che-kays day bee-a-hay

I do not have enough currency
No tengo suficiente cambio
no ten-go soo-fee-thyen-tay kam-bee-o

General phrases and requests

I do not have enough money
No tengo suficiente dinero
*no **ten**-go soo-fee-**thyen**-tay dee-**ne**-ro*

I would like to pay with my credit card
Me gustaría pagar con tarjeta de crédito
*may goo-sta-**ree**-a pa-**gar** kon tar-**hay**-ta day **kre**-dee-to*

Please forward a receipt to this address
Por favor, envíe un recibo a esta dirección
*por fa-**bor**, en-**bee**-ay oon re-**thee**-bo a **es**-ta dee-rek-**thyon***

Please wrap it up for me
Por favor, envuélvamelo
*por fa-**bor**, en-**bwel**-ba-may-lo*

There is no need to wrap it
No hace falta envolverlo
*no **a**-thay **fal**-ta en-bol-**bair**-lo*

Please pack this for shipment
Por favor, envuelva esto para envío
*por fa-**bor**, en-**bwel**-ba **es**-to pa-ra en-**bee**-o*

Will you send it by air freight?
¿Lo enviará por avión?
*lo en-bee-a-**ra** por a-**byon***

Buying groceries

Supermarkets and small grocery stores proliferate, but shopping is more fun in local markets. Most towns and major centres have markets – usually mornings only, Monday to Saturday – with fresh fruit, vegetables and meat at prices that are likely to be lower than those in the shops (and often open to bargaining).

We need to buy some food
Tenemos que comprar comida
*te-**nay**-mos kay kom-**prar** ko-**mee**-da*

I would like — a kilo of potatoes
   Me da — un kilo de patatas
   *may da — oon **kee**-lo day pa-**ta**-tas*

       — a bar of chocolate
       — una barra de chocolate
       *— **oo**-na **ba**-ra day cho-ko-**la**-tay*

       — 100 g of ground coffee
       — cien gramos de café molido
       *— thee-**en gra**-mos day ka-**fay** mo-**lee**-do*

       — two steaks
       — dos filetes
       *— dos fee-**le**-tes*

Buying groceries

— **5 slices of ham**
— cinco lonchas de jamón
— *theen-ko lon-chas day ha-mon*

— **half a dozen eggs**
— media docena de huevos
— *me-dee-a do-thay-na day way-bos*

— **half a kilo of butter**
— medio kilo de mantequilla
— *me-dee-o kee-lo day man-te-kee-ya*

Can I have — **some sugar, please?**
¿Puede darme — azúcar, por favor?
pwe-day dar-may— a-thoo-kar, por fa-bor

— **a bottle of wine, please?**
— una botella de vino, por favor?
— *oo-na bo-te-ya day bee-no, por fa-bor*

— **a kilo of sausages, please?**
— un kilo de salchichas, por favor?
— *oon kee-lo day sal-chee-chas, por fa-bor*

— **a leg of lamb, please?**
— una pierna de cordero, por favor?
— *oo-na pee-air-na day kor-dair-o, por fa-bor*

— **a litre of milk, please?**
— un litro de leche, por favor?
— *oon lee-tro day le-chay, por fa-bor*

Groceries

baby food
comida para bebés
ko-mee-da pa-ra be-bes

biscuits
galletas
ga-yay-tas

bread
pan
pan

butter
mantequilla
man-te-kee-ya

cheese
queso
ke-so

coffee
café
ka-fay

cream
nata
na-ta

eggs
huevos
way-bos

flour
harina
a-ree-na

jam
mermelada
mair-me-la-da

margarine
margarina
mar-ga-ree-na

milk
leche
le-chay

mustard
mostaza
mo-sta-tha

oil
aceite
a-thay-tay

171

Meat and fish

pepper
pimienta
*pee-**myen**-ta*

sugar
azúcar
*a-**thoo**-kar*

rice
arroz
*a-**roth***

tea
té
tay

salt
sal
sal

vinegar
vinagre
*bee-**na**-gray*

soup
sopa
so-pa

yoghurt
yogur
*yo-**goor***

Meat and fish

beef
carne de vaca
kar-nay day ba-ka

fish
pescado
*pe-**ska**-do*

chicken
pollo
po-yo

ham
jamón
*ha-**mon***

cod
bacalao
*ba-ka-**la**-o*

herring
arenque
*a-**ren**-kay*

172

kidneys
riñones
*reen-**yo**-nes*

mussels
mejillones
*me-hee-**yo**-nes*

lamb
cordero
*kor-**dair**-o*

pork
cerdo
***thair**-do*

liver
hígado
***ee**-ga-do*

sole
lenguado
*len-**gwa**-do*

meat
carne
***kar**-nay*

veal
ternera
*tair-**nair**-a*

At the newsagent's

English newspapers are readily available in major cities and tourist resort areas. They are generally a day late, and the quality dailies are expensive. You can get cheaper, locally published, English-language papers in many resort areas.

Do you sell — English paperbacks?
   ¿Vende — libros de bolsillo en inglés?
   ben**-day — **lee**-bros day bol-**see**-yo en een-**gles

   — postcards?
   — postales?
   — *po-**sta**-les*

173

At the newsagent's

— **a local map?**
— un plano de la localidad?
— *oon pla-no day la lo-ka-lee-dad*

— **a road map?**
— un mapa de carreteras?
— *oon ma-pa day ka-re-tair-as*

— **coloured pencils?**
— lápices de color?
— *la-pee-thes day ko-lor*

— **drawing paper?**
— papel de dibujo?
— *pa-pel day dee-boo-ho*

— **felt pens?**
— rotuladores?
— *ro-too-la-do-res*

— **street maps?**
— planos de ciudad?
— *pla-nos day thee-oo-dad*

I would like some postage stamps
Me da sellos de correos
may da se-yos day ko-ray-os

Do you have — English books?
¿Tiene — libros en inglés?
tee-e-nay — lee-bros en een-gles

At the newsagent's

— **English newspapers?**
— periódicos en inglés?
— *pe-ree-o-dee-kos en een-gles*

I need — **some writing paper**
Necesito — papel de cartas
ne-the-see-to — *pa-pel day kar-tas*

— **a bottle of ink**
— una botella de tinta
— *oo-na bo-te-ya day teen-ta*

— **a pen**
— un bolígrafo
— *oon bo-lee-gra-fo*

— **a pencil**
— un lápiz
— *oon la-peeth*

— **some adhesive tape**
— cinta adhesiva
— *theen-ta a-de-see-ba*

— **some envelopes**
— sobres
— *so-bres*

At the tobacconist's

Do you have — cigarette papers?
    ¿Tiene — papel de fumar?
tee-e-nay — *pa-pel day foo-mar*

    — a box of matches
    — una caja de cerillas
    — *oo-na ka-ha day the-ree-yas*

    — a cigar
    — un cigarro
    — *oon thee-ga-ro*

    — a cigarette lighter
    — un mechero
    — *oon me-chair-o*

    — a gas (butane) refill
    — una carga de gas
    — *oo-na kar-ga day gas*

    — a pipe
    — una pipa
    — *oo-na pee-pa*

    — a pouch of pipe tobacco
    — una petaca de tabaco de pipa
    — *oo-na pe-ta-ka day ta-ba-ko day pee-pa*

— some pipe cleaners
— unos limpiapipas
— *oo-nos leem-pya-pee-pas*

Have you got — any American brands?
¿Tiene — marcas americanas?
tee-e-nay — mar-kas a-me-ree-ka-nas

— any English brands?
— marcas inglesas?
— *mar-kas een-glay-sas*

— rolling tobacco?
— tabaco de liar?
— *ta-ba-ko day lee-ar*

A packet of … please
Un paquete de … por favor
oon pa-ke-tay day … por fa-bor

— with filter tips
— con filtro
— *kon feel-tro*

— without filters
— sin filtro
— *seen feel-tro*

At the chemist's

As in Britain, you can get drugs from a chemist (*farmacia*) during shopping hours. Rotas of chemists open at other times are posted in their windows and published in local papers.

Do you have toothpaste?
¿Tiene pasta de dientes?
tee-e-nay pa-sta day dee-en-tes

I need some high-protection suntan cream
Necesito una crema solar de alta protección
ne-the-see-to oo-na kray-ma so-lar day al-ta pro-tek-thyon

Can you give me something for — a headache?
¿Puede darme algo para
pwe-day dar-may al-go pa-ra
— el dolor de cabeza?
— *el do-lor day ka-bay-tha*

— insect bites
— las picaduras de insectos?
— *las pee-ka-doo-ras day een-sek-tos*

— a cold
— un catarro
— *oon ka-ta-ro*

— a cough
— tos
— *tos*

At the chemist's

— **a sore throat**
— dolor de garganta
— *do-lor* day gar-*gan*-ta

— **an upset stomach**
— mal del estómago
— *mal del e-sto-ma-go*

— **toothache**
— dolor de muelas
— *do-lor* day *mway*-las

— **hay fever**
— fiebre del heno
— *fee-e-bray del ay*-no

— **sunburn**
— quemadura de sol
— *ke-ma-doo-ra* day sol

Do I need a prescription?
¿Necesito una receta?
ne-the-see-to oo-na re-thay-ta

How many do I take?
¿Cuántas tengo que tomar?
kwan-tas ten-go kay to-mar

How often do I take them?
¿Con qué frecuencia tengo que tomarlas?
kon kay fre-kwen-thee-a ten-go kay to-mar-las

Medicines and toiletries

Are they safe for children to take?
¿Los niños pueden tomarlas sin riesgo?
*los **neen**-yos **pwe**-den to-**mar**-las seen ree-**ez**-go*

Medicines and toiletries

antihistamine
antihistamínico
*an-tee-ee-sta-**mee**-nee-ko*

antiseptic
antiséptico
*an-tee-**sep**-tee-ko*

aspirin
aspirina
*a-spee-**ree**-na*

bandage
vendaje
*ben-**da**-hay*

bubble bath
espuma de baño
*e-**spoo**-ma day **ban**-yo*

cleansing milk
leche limpiadora
*le-chay leem-pya-**do**-ra*

conditioner
suavizante
*swa-bee-**than**-tay*

condom
preservativo
*pray-sair-ba-**tee**-bo*

contraceptive
anticonceptivo
*an-tee-kon-thep-**tee**-bo*

cotton wool
algodón hidrófilo
*al-go-**don** ee-**dro**-fee-lo*

deodorant
desodorante
*des-o-do-**ran**-tay*

disinfectant
desinfectante
*des-een-fek-**tan**-tay*

Medicines and toiletries

eau de Cologne
agua de colonia
a-gwa day ko-lon-ya

eye shadow
sombra de ojos
som-bra day o-hos

face powder
polvos
pol-bos

hair spray
laca para el cabello
la-ka pa-ra el ka-be-yo

hand cream
crema de manos
kray-ma day ma-nos

insect repellent
repelente de insectos
ray-pe-len-tay day een-sek-tos

laxative
laxante
lak-san-tay

lipstick
barra de labios
ba-ra day la-bee-os

mascara
rímel
ree-mel

moisturiser
loción hidratante
lo-thyon ee-dra-tan-tay

mouthwash
antiséptico bucal
an-tee-sep-tee-ko boo-kal

nail file
lima de uñas
lee-ma day oon-yas

nail varnish
esmalte de uñas
es-mal-tay day oon-yas

nail varnish remover
quitaesmalte
kee-ta-es-mal-tay

perfume
perfume
pair-foo-may

plasters
tiritas
tee-ree-tas

Shopping for clothes

razor blades
hojas de afeitar
o-has day a-fay-tar

sanitary towels
compresas
kom-pray-sas

shampoo
champú
cham-poo

shaving cream
espuma de afeitar
es-poo-ma day a-fay-tar

soap
jabón
ha-bon

suntan lotion
bronceador
bron-thay-a-dor

talc
talco
tal-ko

tampons
tampones
tam-po-nays

tissues
Kleenex
klee-neks

toilet water
colonia
ko-lon-ya

toothpaste
pasta de dientes
pa-sta day dee-en-tes

Shopping for clothes

I am just looking, thank you
Sólo estoy mirando, gracias
so-lo es-toy mee-ran-do, gra-thee-as

Shopping for clothes

I do not like it
No me gusta
*no may **goo**-sta*

I like it
Me gusta
*may **goo**-sta*

I will take it
Lo llevaré
*lo ye-ba-**ray***

I like — this one
Me gusta — éste
*may **goo**-sta — **es**-tay*

— that one there
— aquél
*— a-**kel***

— the one in the window
— el que está en el escaparate
*— el kay es-**ta** en el e-ska-pa-**ra**-tay*

I would like — this suit
Quiero comprar — este traje
*kee-**e**-ro kom-**prar** — **es**-tay **tra**-hay*

— this hat
— este sombrero
*— **es**-tay som-**brair**-o*

183

Shopping for clothes

I would like one — with a zip
Quisiera uno — con cremallera
ke-see-air-a oo-no — kon kre-ma-yair-a

— without a belt
— sin cinturón
— *seen then-too-ron*

Can you please measure me?
¿Puede medirme, por favor?
pwe-day me-deer-may, por fa-bor

Can I change it if it does not fit?
¿Puedo cambiarlo si no me vale?
pwe-do kam-byar-lo see no may ba-lay

Have you got this in other colours?
¿Tiene éste en otros colores?
tee-e-nay es-tay en o-tros ko-lo-res

I take a large shoe size
Uso una talla de zapato grande
oo-so oo-na ta-ya day tha-pa-to gran-day

I take continental size 40
Uso la talla cuarenta europea
oo-so la ta-ya kwa-ren-ta ay-oo-ro-pay-a

Is it too long?
¿Es demasiado largo?
es de-ma-sya-do lar-go

184

Shopping for clothes

Is it too short?
¿Es demasiado corto?
es de-ma-sya-do kor-to

Is there a full-length mirror?
¿Hay algún espejo de cuerpo entero?
eye al-goon es-pe-ho day kwair-po en-tair-o

Is this all you have?
¿Es esto todo lo que tiene?
es es-to to-do lo kay tee-e-nay

It does not fit
No me vale
no may ba-lay

It does not suit me
No me queda bien
no may kay-da byen

May I see it in daylight?
¿Puedo verlo a la luz del día?
pwe-do bair-lo a la looth del dee-a

Where are the changing (dressing) rooms?
¿Dónde están los probadores?
don-day es-tan los pro-ba-do-res

Where can I try it on?
¿Dónde puedo probármelo?
don-day pwe-do pro-bar-may-lo

185

Shopping for clothes

Have you got — a large size?
  ¿Tiene — una talla grande?
  *tee-e-nay — **oo**-na **ta**-ya **gran**-day*

  — a small size?
  — una talla pequeña?
  — ***oo**-na **ta**-ya pe-**ken**-ya*

What is it made of?
¿De qué material es?
*day kay ma-te-ree-**al** es*

Is it guaranteed?
¿Tiene garantía?
*tee-e-nay ga-ran-**tee**-a*

Will it shrink?
¿Encogerá?
*en-ko-hair-**a***

Is it drip-dry?
¿Es de lava y pon?
*es day **la**-ba ee pon*

Is it dry-clean only?
¿Es de limpiar en seco sólamente?
*es day leem-**pyar** en **se**-ko so-la-**men**-tay*

Is it machine washable?
¿Es lavable a máquina?
*es la-**ba**-blay a **ma**-kee-na*

186

Clothes and accessories

acrylic
acrílico
*a-**kree**-lee-ko*

belt
cinturón
*theen-too-**ron***

blouse
blusa
***bloo**-sa*

bra
sujetador
*soo-he-ta-**dor***

bracelet
pulsera
*pool-**say**-ra*

brooch
broche
***bro**-chay*

button
botón
*bo-**ton***

cardigan
chaqueta de punto
*cha-**kay**-ta day **poon**-to*

coat
abrigo
*a-**bree**-go*

corduroy
pana
***pa**-na*

cotton
algodón
*al-go-**don***

denim
tela vaquera
***tay**-la ba-**kair**-a*

dress
vestido
*be-**stee**-do*

dungarees
pantalón de peto
*pan-ta-**lon** day **pay**-to*

Clothes and accessories

earrings
pendientes
*pen-dee-**en**-tes*

espadrilles
alpargatas
*al-**par**-ga-tas*

fur
piel
pyel

gloves
guantes
gwan-tes

handbag
bolso
***bol**-so*

handkerchief
pañuelo
*pan-yoo-**ay**-lo*

hat
sombrero
*som-**brair**-o*

jacket
chaqueta
*cha-**kay**-ta*

jeans
vaqueros
*ba-**kair**-os*

jersey
jersey
*hair-**say***

lace
encaje
*en-**ka**-hay*

leather
cuero
***kwair**-o*

linen
lino
***lee**-no*

necklace
collar
*ko-**yar***

nightdress
camisón
*ka-mee-**son***

nylon
nylon
*nee-**lon***

Clothes and accessories

pants (women's)
bragas
bra-gas

petticoat
combinación
kom-bee-na-thyon

polyester
poliéster
po-lee-e-stair

pullover
pulóver
poo-lo-bair

purse
monedero
mo-ne-dair-o

pyjamas
pijama
pee-ha-ma

raincoat
impermeable
eem-pair-may-a-blay

ring
anillo
a-nee-yo

sandals
sandalias
san-da-lee-as

scarf
bufanda
boo-fan-da

shirt
camisa
ka-mee-sa

shoes
zapatos
tha-pa-tos

shorts
pantalón corto
pan-ta-lon kor-to

silk
seda
say-da

skirt
falda
fal-da

slip
enagua
e-na-gwa

Clothes and accessories

socks
calcetines
*kal-the-**tee**-nes*

stockings
medias
me-dee-as

suede
ante
***an**-tay*

suit (men's)
traje
***tra**-hay*

suit (women's)
traje de chaqueta
***tra**-hay day cha-**kay**-ta*

sweater
suéter
***swe**-tair*

swimming trunks
bañador
*ban-ya-**dor***

swimsuit
traje de baño
***tra**-hay day **ban**-yo*

T-shirt
camiseta
*ka-mee-**say**-ta*

terylene
terylene
*te-ree-**le**-nay*

tie
corbata
*kor-**ba**-ta*

tights
medias
***me**-dee-as*

towel
toalla
*to-**a**-ya*

trousers
pantalón
*pan-ta-**lon***

umbrella
paraguas
*pa-**ra**-gwas*

underpants (men's)
calzoncillos
*kal-thon-**thee**-yos*

velvet
terciopelo
tair-thee-o-pe-lo

vest
camiseta
ka-mee-say-ta

wallet
cartera
kar-tair-a

watch
reloj
re-loh

wool
lana
la-na

zip
cremallera
kre-ma-yair-a

Photography

I need a film — for this camera
Quiero una película — para esta cámara
kee-e-ro oo-na pe-lee-koo-la — pa-ra es-ta ka-ma-ra

— for this camcorder
— para este camcórder
— pa-ra es-tay kam-kor-dair

— for this cine-camera
— para esta cámara de cine
— pa-ra es-ta ka-ma-ra day thee-nay

— for this video camera
— para este videocámara
— pa-ra e s-tay bee-day-o-ka-ma-ra

Photography

Can you develop this film, please?
¿Puede revelar esta película, por favor?
pwe-day re-be-lar es-ta pe-lee-koo-la, por fa-bor

I would like this photo enlarged
Quiero que amplíen esta foto
kee-e-ro kay am-plee-en es-ta fo-to

I would like two prints of this one
Quiero dos copias de ésta
kee-e-ro dos ko-pyas day es-ta

When will the photos be ready?
¿Cuándo estarán las fotos?
kwan-do es-ta-ran las fo-tos

I want — a black and white film
Quiero — una película en blanco y negro
kee-e-ro — oo-na pe-lee-koo-la en blan-ko ee ne-gro

— a colour print film
— una película en color
— oo-na pe-lee-koo-la en ko-lor

— a colour slide film
— una película de diapositivas en color
— oo-na pe-lee-koo-la day dee-a-po-zee-tee-bas en ko-lor

— batteries for the flash
— pilas para el flash
— pee-las pa-ra el flas

Camera repairs

I am having trouble with my camera
Tengo un problema con la cámara
*ten-go oon pro-**blay**-ma kon la **ka**-ma-ra*

The film is jammed
La película está atascada
*la pe-**lee**-koo-la es-**ta** a-ta-**ska**-da*

There is something wrong with my camera
Le ocurre algo a mi cámara
*lay o-**koo**-ray **al**-go a mee **ka**-ma-ra*

Where can I get my camera repaired?
¿Dónde puedo llevar la cámara a reparar?
*don-day **pwe**-do **ye**-bar la **ka**-ma-ra a re-pa-**rar***

Camera parts

accessory
accesorio
*ak-the-**so**-ree-o*

blue filter
filtro azul
*feel-tro a-**thool***

camcorder
camcórder
*kam-**kor**-dair*

cartridge
carrete
*ka-**re**-tay*

Camera parts

cassette
cassette
ka-se-tay

cine-camera
cámara de cine
ka-ma-ra day thee-nay

distance
distancia
dee-stan-thee-a

enlargement
ampliación
am-plee-a-thyon

exposure
exposición
ek-spo-zee-thyon

exposure meter
fotómetro
fo-to-me-tro

flash
flash
flas

flash bulb
bombilla de flash
bom-bee-ya day flas

flash cube
cubo de flash
koo-bo day flas

focal distance
distancia focal
dee-stan-thee-a fo-kal

focus
foco
fo-ko

image
imagen
ee-ma-hen

in focus
enfocado
en-fo-ka-do

lens cover
tapa de objetivo
ta-pa day ob-he-tee-bo

lens
objetivo
ob-he-tee-bo

negative
negativo
ne-ga-tee-bo

194

out of focus
desenfocado
des-en-fo-ka-do

over-exposed
sobreexpuesto
so-bray-eks-pwes-to

picture
fotografía
fo-to-gra-fee-a

print
copia
ko-pya

projector
proyector
pro-yek-tor

red filter
filtro rojo
feel-tro ro-ho

reel
rollo
ro-yo

shade
sombra
som-bra

shutter
obturador
ob-too-ra-dor

shutter speed
velocidad de obturación
be-lo-thee-dad day ob-too-ra-thyon

slide
diapositiva
dee-a-po-zee-tee-ba

transparency
transparencia
trans-pa-ren-thee-a

tripod
trípode
tree-po-day

viewfinder
visor
bee-sor

wide-angle lens
granangular
gra-nan-goo-lar

yellow filter
filtro amarillo
feel-tro a-ma-ree-yo

195

At the hairdresser's

I would like to make an appointment
Quisiera reservar hora
*kee-see-**air**-a re-sair-**bar** o-ra*

 I want — a haircut
 Quiero — cortarme el pelo
*kee-e-ro — kor-**tar**-may el **pelo***

       — a trim
       — cortarme las puntas
       *— kor-**tar**-may las **poon**-tas*

Not too much off
No quite demasiado
*no **kee**-tay de-ma-**sya**-do*

Take a little more off the back
Quite un poco más por detrás
kee**-tay oon **po**-ko mas por de-**tras

       Please cut my hair — short
       Por favor, córteme el pelo — corto
*por fa-**bor**, **kor**-tay-may el **pe**-lo — **kor**-to*

       — fairly short
       — bastante corto
       *— ba-**stan**-tay **kor**-to*

At the hairdresser's

— **in a fringe**
— con flequillo
— *kon fle-**kee**-yo*

That is fine, thank you
Está bien, gracias
*es-ta byen, **gra**-thee-as*

I would like — **a perm**
Quisiera — una permanente
*kee-see-**air**-ra* — *oo-na pair-ma-**nen**-tay*

— **a blow-dry**
— secar con secador
— *se-**kar** kon se-ka-**dor***

— **my hair dyed**
— teñirme el pelo
— *ten-**yeer**-may el **pe**-lo*

— **my hair streaked**
— mechas en el pelo
— ***may**-chas en el **pe**-lo*

— **a shampoo and cut**
— lavar y cortar
— *la-**bar** ee kor-**tar***

— **a shampoo and set**
— lavar y marcar
— *la-**bar** ee mar-**kar***

Laundry

> **— a conditioner**
> — un suavizante
> — *oon swa-bee-than-tay*

> **— hair spray**
> — laca de pelo
> — *la-ka day pe-lo*

The dryer is too hot
El secador está demasiado caliente
el se-ka-dor es-ta de-ma-sya-do ka-lee-en-tay

The water is too hot
El agua está demasiado caliente
el a-gwa es-ta de-ma-sya-do ka-lee-en-tay

Laundry

Is there a launderette nearby?
¿Hay alguna lavandería cercana?
eye al-goo-na la-ban-de-ree-a thair-ka-na

How does the washing machine work?
¿Cómo funciona la lavadora?
ko-mo foon-thyo-na la la-ba-do-ra

How long will it take?
¿Cuánto tardará?
kwan-to tar-da-ra

Can you — clean this skirt?
¿Me puede — limpiar esta falda?
*may **pwe**-day— leem-**pyar** es-ta **fal**-da*

— clean and press these shirts?
— limpiar y planchar estas camisas?
— *leem-**pyar** ee plan-**char** es-tas ka-**mee**-sas*

— wash these clothes?
— lavar esta ropa?
— *la-**bar** es-ta **ro**-pa*

This stain is — oil
Esta mancha es — de aceite
*es-ta **man**-cha es — day a-**thay**-ee-tay*

— blood
— de sangre
— *day **san**-gray*

— coffee
— de café
— *day ka-**fay***

— ink
— de tinta
— *day **teen**-ta*

This fabric is delicate
Esta tela es delicada
*es-ta **tay**-la es de-lee-**ka**-da*

General repairs

I have lost my dry cleaning ticket
He perdido el resguardo de la tintorería
*ay pair-**dee**-do el rez-**gwar**-do day la teen-to-re-**ree**-a*

Please send it to this address
Por favor, enviélo a esta dirección
*por fa-**bor**, en-**bee**-ay-lo a **es**-ta dee-rek-**thyon***

When will I come back?
¿Cuándo puedo volver?
kwan**-do **pwe**-do bol-**bair

When will my clothes be ready?
¿Cuándo estará mi ropa lista?
***kwan**-do es-ta-**ra** mee **ro**-pa **lee**-sta*

I will come back — later
   Volveré — más tarde
  *bol-bair-**ay** — mas **tar**-day*

     — in an hour
     — dentro de una hora
     *— **den**-tro day **oo**-na **o**-ra*

General repairs

 This is — broken
 Esto está — roto
***es**-to es-**ta** — **ro**-to*

General repairs

- **damaged**
- averiado
- *a-be-ree-a-do*

- **torn**
- estropeado
- *e-stro-pay-a-do*

Can you repair it?
¿Puede repararlo?
pwe-day re-pa-rar-lo

Can you do it quickly?
¿Puede hacerlo rápidamente?
pwe-day a-thair-lo ra-pee-da-men-tay

Have you got a spare part for this?
¿Tiene alguna pieza de repuesto para esto?
tee-e-nay al-goo-na pee-ay-tha day re-pwe-sto pa-ra es-to

Would you have a look at this please?
¿Puede mirar esto, por favor?
pwe-day mee-rar es-to, por fa-bor

Here is the guarantee
Aquí está la garantía
a-kee es-ta la ga-ran-tee-a

At the post office

Post offices (*oficinas de correos*) are open in the mornings and again from 5.00pm to 7.00pm Monday to Friday and on Saturday mornings. They can be found in most centres. Stamps (*sellos*) are also available from tobacconists (*estancos*) and from hotels.

12 stamps please
Doce sellos, por favor
*do-thay **se**-yos, por fa-**bor***

I need to send this by courier
Necesito enviar esto por servicio de mensajero
*ne-the-**see**-to en-**byar** es-to por sair-**bee**-thee-o day
  men-sa-**hair**-o*

I want to send a telegram
Quiero enviar este telegrama
*kee-**e**-ro en-**byar** es-tay te-le-**gra**-ma*

I want to send this by registered mail
Quiero enviar esto por correo certificado
*kee-**e**-ro en-**byar** es-to por ko-**ray**-o thair-tee-fee-**ka**-do*

I want to send this parcel
Quiero enviar este paquete
*kee-**e**-ro en-**byar** es-tay pa-**ke**-tay*

202

When will it arrive?
¿Cuándo llegará?
kwan-do ye-ga-ra

> **How much is a letter — to Britain?**
> ¿Cuánto cuesta una carta — a Gran Bretaña?
> *kwan-to kwes-ta oo-na kar-ta — a gran bre-tan-ya*

> **— to the United States?**
> — a los Estados Unidos?
> — *a los e-sta-dos oo-nee-dos*

Can I have six stamps for postcards to Britain?
Me da seis sellos para postales a Gran Bretaña
may da says se-yos pa-ra po-sta-les a gran bre-tan-ya

Can I have a telegram form, please?
¿Puede darme un impreso de telegrama, por favor?
pwe-day dar-may oon eem-pray-so day te-le-gra-ma, por fa-bor

Using the telephone

Most phone numbers have six digits, usually written in three groups of two. Madrid, Barcelona and a number of other towns have seven-digit numbers.

The ringing tone on Spanish phones is a slowly repeating long tone rather than a double ring.

Area codes, which you dial before the local number when

Using the telephone

calling one area from another, have two or three digits, the first of which is always 9.

To phone Spain, dial 00 34 to access the country, then dial the area code, leaving off the initial 9. Then dial the local number.

To phone Britain from Spain, dial 07 and wait for a high-pitched tone before dialling the country code, which for Britain is 44. Then dial the British area code without the first 0, then your number.

Most public phones have a groove on top to hold coins and a digital display of how much credit remains. Calling from a public phone is far cheaper than calling from a hotel bedroom – hotels are entitled to make a heavy service charge. In big cities, you can also make calls from central telephone offices (*locutorios*), where you pay for the call – plus a service charge – after you have made it.

Can I use the telephone, please?
¿Puedo utilizar el teléfono, por favor?
pwe-do oo-tee-lee-thar el te-le-fo-no, por fa-bor

Can I dial direct?
¿Puedo marcar directamente?
pwe-do mar-kar dee-rek-ta-men-tay

Can you connect me with the international operator?
¿Puede conectarme con la operadora internacional?
pwe-day ko-nek-tar-may kon la o-pe-ra-do-ra
  een-tair-na-thyo-nal

Using the telephone

Have you got any change?
¿Tiene cambio?
tee-e-nay kam-bee-o

How do I use the telephone?
¿Cómo se utiliza el teléfono?
ko-mo say oo-tee-lee-tha el te-le-fo-no

How much is it to phone to London?
¿Cuánto cuesta llamar a Londres?
kwan-to kwes-ta ya-mar a lon-dres

I must make a phone call to Britain
Tengo que llamar a Gran Bretaña
ten-go kay ya-mar a gran bre-tan-ya

I need to make a phone call
Tengo que hacer una llamada
ten-go kay a-thair oo-na ya-ma-da

What is the code for the UK?
¿Cuál es el código del Reino Unido?
kwal es el ko-dee-go del ray-no oo-nee-do

I would like to make a reversed charge call
Deseo hacer una llamada a cobro revertido
de-say-o a-thair oo-na ya-ma-da a ko-bro re-bair-tee-do

The number I need is...
El número que necesito es...
el noo-me-o kay ne-the-see-to es...

What you may hear

What is the charge?
¿Cuánto es?
kwan-to es

Please, call me back
Por favor, devuelva mi llamada
por fa-bor, de-bwel-ba mee ya-ma-da

I am sorry. We were cut off
Lo siento. Se ha cortado
lo syen-to. Say a kor-ta-do

What you may hear

El número no funciona
el noo-me-ro no foon-thyo-na
The number is out of order

Está comunicando
es-ta ko-moo-nee-kan-do
The line is engaged (busy)

Estoy intentando conectarle
es-toy een-ten-tan-do ko-nek-tar-lay
I am trying to connect you

Hable, por favor
a-blay, por fa-bor
Please go ahead

Hola, soy el director
*o-la, soy el dee-rek-**tor***
Hello, this is the manager

Le voy a pasar con el señor Smith
*lay boy a pa-**sar** kon el sen-**yor** Smith*
I am putting you through to Mr Smith

No puedo obtener este número
*no **pwe**-do ob-te-**nair** es-tay **noo**-me-ro*
I cannot obtain this number

Changing money

Banks are open Monday to Friday from 8.30am to 2.00pm
and on Saturdays from 9.00am until 1.00pm.

Can I contact my bank to arrange for a transfer?
¿Puedo contactar a mi banco para pedir una transferencia?
***pwe**-do kon-tak-**tar** a mee **ban**-ko **pa**-ra pe-**deer oo**-na*
  *trans-fe-**ren**-thee-a*

Has my cash arrived?
¿Ha llegado mi dinero?
*a ye-**ga**-do mee dee-**ne**-ro*

I would like to obtain a cash advance with my credit card
Quisiera un anticipo en metálico con mi tarjeta de crédito
*kee-see-**air**-ra oon an-tee-**thee**-po en me-**ta**-lee-ko kon mee*
  *tar-**hay**-ta day **kre**-dee-to*

Changing money

This is the name and address of my bank
Éste es el nombre y la dirección de mi banco
*es-tay es el **nom**-bray ee la dee-rek-**thyon** day mee **ban**-ko*

   Can I change — these traveller's cheques?
¿Puedo cambiar — estos cheques de viaje?
*pwe-do kam-**byar** — **es**-tos **che**-kays day bee-a-**hay***

           — these notes (bills)?
         — estos billetes?
         *— **es**-tos bee-**ye**-tes*

Here is my passport
Aquí tiene mi pasaporte
*a-**kee** tee-e-nay mee pa-sa-**por**-tay*

What is the rate of exchange?
¿A cuánto está el cambio?
*a **kwan**-to es-**ta** el **kam**-bee-o*

   What is the rate for — sterling?
   ¿A cuánto está el cambio — de la libra esterlina?
*a **kwan**-to es-**ta** el **kam**-bee-o — day la **lee**-bra es-tair-**lee**-na*

               — dollars?
             — del dólar?
             *— del **do**-lar*

What is your commission?
¿Cuánto es la comisión?
*kwan-to es la ko-mee-**syon***

208

HEALTH

To receive medical treatment under the Spanish health service, you will need to get an E111 form from a post office before you travel. Take a photocopy of it and, if you need treatment, show the doctor the original and hand over the copy. Even if you do have an E111, you should not go without travel insurance.

As in Britain, you can get drugs from a chemist during shopping hours. Rotas of chemists open at other times are posted in their windows and published in local newspapers.

All dental treatment is private; your travel insurance may cover emergency treatment.

In an emergency, call the operator for a telephone number; your accommodation may also be able to help. If you need urgent hospital treatment, E111 arrangements entitle you to treatment in public wards of state hospitals. Show your E111 form immediately to avoid being charged.

What's wrong?

I need a doctor
Necesito un médico
*ne-the-**see**-to oon **me**-dee-ko*

What's wrong?

Can I see a doctor?
¿Puedo ver a un médico?
pwe-do bair a oon me-dee-ko

He / she is hurt
Está herido / herida
es-ta e-ree-do / e-ree-da

He / she has been badly injured
Está malherido / malherida
es-ta mal-e-ree-do / mal-e-ree-da

He / she has burnt himself / herself
Se ha quemado
say a ke-ma-do

He / she has dislocated his / her shoulder
Se ha dislocado el hombro
say a dees-lo-ka-do el om-bro

He / she is unconscious
Está inconsciente
es-ta een-kons-thee-en-tay

He / she has a temperature
Tiene fiebre
tee-e-nay fee-e-bray

He / she has been bitten
Tiene una mordedura
tee-e-nay oo-na mor-de-doo-ra

My son has cut himself
Mi hijo se ha hecho cortado
mee ee-ho say a e-cho kor-ta-do

My son is ill
Mi hijo está enfermo
mee ee-ho es-ta en-fair-mo

I am ill
Estoy enfermo / enferma
es-toy en-fair-mo / en-fair-ma

I am a diabetic
Soy diabético / diabética
soy dee-a-be-tee-ko / dee-a-be-tee-ka

I am allergic to penicillin
Soy alérgico / alérgica a la penicilina
soy a-lair-hee-ko / a-lair-hee-ka a la pe-nee-thee-lee-na

I am badly sunburnt
Tengo quemaduras de sol
ten-go ke-ma-doo-ras day sol

I am constipated
Estoy estreñido / estreñida
es-toy es-tren-yee-do / es-tren-yee-da

I cannot sleep
No puedo dormir
no pwe-do dor-meer

What's wrong?

I feel dizzy
Estoy mareado / mareada
*es-**toy** ma-ray-**a**-do / ma-ray-**a**-da*

I feel faint
Me siento mareado / mareada
*may **syen**-to ma-ray-**a**-do / ma-ray-**a**-da*

I feel nauseous
Siento náuseas
*syen-to **now**-say-as*

I fell
Me he caído
*may ay ka-**ee**-do*

I have a pain here
Me duele aquí
*may **dwe**-lay a-**kee***

I have a rash here
Tengo un sarpullido aquí
*ten-go oon sar-poo-**yee**-do a-**kee***

I have been sick
He estado vomitando
*ay es-**ta**-do bo-mee-**tan**-do*

I have been stung
Tengo una picadura
*ten-go **oo**-na pee-ka-**doo**-ra*

I have cut myself
Me he cortado
*may ay kor-**ta**-do*

I have diarrhoea
Tengo diarrea
***ten**-go dee-a-**ray**-a*

I have pulled a muscle
Tengo un tirón en un músculo
***ten**-go oon tee-**ron** en oon **moo**-skoo-lo*

I have sunstroke
Tengo insolación
ten**-go een-so-la-**thyon

I suffer from high blood pressure
Tengo la tensión alta
***ten**-go la ten-**syon al**-ta*

I think I have food poisoning
Creo que tengo una intoxicación de alimentos
***kray**-o kay **ten**-go **oo**-na een-tok-see-ka-**thyon** day a-lee-**men**-tos*

It is inflamed here
Esto está inflamado
*es-to es-**ta** een-fla-**ma**-do*

My arm is broken
Me he roto el brazo
*may ay **ro**-to el **bra**-tho*

What's wrong?

My stomach is upset
Tengo mal de estómago
ten-go mal day e-sto-ma-go

My tongue is coated
Tengo la lengua sucia
ten-go la len-gwa soo-thya

There is a swelling here
Tengo hinchazón aquí
ten-go een-cha-thon a-kee

      I have hurt — my arm
    Me he hecho daño en — el brazo
may ay e-cho dan-yo en— el bra-tho

            — my leg
            — la pierna
            — la pee-air-na

    It is painful — to walk
    Me duele al — caminar
may dwe-lay al— ka-mee-nar

            — to breathe
            — respirar
            — re-spee-rar

            — to swallow
            — tragar
            — tra-gar

What's wrong

I have — a headache
Tengo — dolor de cabeza
ten-go — *do-**lor** day ka-**bay**-tha*

> **— a sore throat**
> — dolor de garganta
> — *do-**lor** day gar-**gan**-ta*

> **— an earache**
> — dolor de oído
> — *do-**lor** day o-**ee**-do*

I am taking these drugs
Estoy tomando estos medicamentos
*es-**toy** to-**man**-do es-tos me-dee-ka-**men**-tos*

Can you give me a prescription for them?
¿Puede hacerme una receta para ellos?
*pwe-day **dar**-may **oo**-na re-**thay**-ta **pa**-ra e-yos*

I am on the pill
Estoy tomando la píldora
*es-**toy** to-**man**-do la **peel**-do-ra*

I am pregnant
Estoy embarazada
*es-**toy** em-ba-ra-**tha**-da*

My blood group is ...
Mi grupo sanguíneo es ...
*mee **groo**-po san-**gee**-nay-o es ...*

At the hospital

I do not know my blood group
No sé el grupo sanguíneo que tengo
*no say el **groo**-po san-**gee**-nay-o kay **ten**-go*

I need some antibiotics
Necesito antibióticos
*ne-the-**see**-to an-tee-bee-**o**-tee-kos*

Do I have to go into hospital?
¿Tengo que ir al hospital?
*ten-go kay eer al o-spee-**tal***

Do I need an operation?
¿Tengo que operarme?
*ten-go kay o-pe-**rar**-may*

At the hospital

Here is my E-111 form
Aquí está mi formulario E-111 (ciento once)
*a-**kee** es-**ta** mee for-moo-**la**-ree-o thee-**en**-to **on**-thay*

How do I get reimbursed?
¿Cómo me van a reembolsar?
*ko-mo may ban a ray-em-bol-**sar***

Must I stay in bed?
¿Tengo que estar en la cama?
*ten-go kay es-**tar** en la **ka**-ma*

When will I be able to travel?
¿Cuándo podré viajar?
kwan-*do po-**dray** bee-a-**har***

Will I be able to go out tomorrow?
¿Podré salir mañana?
*po-**dray** sa-**leer** man-**ya**-na*

Parts of the body

ankle
tobillo
*to-**bee**-yo*

arm
brazo
***bra**-tho*

back
espalda
*es-**pal**-da*

bone
hueso
***we**-so*

breast
pecho
***pe**-cho*

cheek
mejilla
*me-**hee**-ya*

chest
pecho
***pe**-cho*

ear
oreja
*o-**ray**-ha*

elbow
codo
***ko**-do*

eye
ojo
***o**-ho*

217

Parts of the body

face
cara
ka-ra

finger
dedo
de-do

foot
pie
pee-ay

hand
mano
ma-no

heart
corazón
ko-ra-thon

kidney
riñon
reen-yon

knee
rodilla
ro-dee-ya

leg
pierna
pee-air-na

liver
hígado
ee-ga-do

lungs
pulmones
pool-mo-nes

mouth
boca
bo-ka

muscle
músculo
moos-koo-lo

neck
cuello
kwe-yo

nose
nariz
na-reeth

skin
piel
pyel

stomach
estómago
e-sto-ma-go

throat
garganta
gar-gan-ta

wrist
muñeca
moon-yay-ka

At the dentist's

I have to see the dentist
Tengo que ir al dentista
ten-go kay eer al den-tee-sta

I have a toothache
Tengo dolor de muelas
ten-go do-lor day mway-las

Are you going to fill it?
¿Va a empastarme?
ba a em-pa-star-may

I have broken a tooth
Me ha roto una muela
may a ro-to oo-na mway-la

Will you have to take it out?
¿Tendrá que sacármela?
ten-dra kay sa-kar-may-la

My false teeth are broken
Se me han roto los dientes postizos
say may an ro-to los dee-en-tes po-stee-thos

At the dentist's

Can you repair them?
¿Puede reparármelos?
*pwe-day re-pa-**rar**-may-los*

My gums are sore
Me duelen las encías
*may **dwe**-len las en-**thee**-as*

Please give me an injection
Póngame una inyección, por favor
pon**-ga-may **oo**-na een-yek-**thyon**, por fa-**bor

That hurts
Eso duele
*e-so **dwe**-lay*

The filling has come out
Se me ha caído el empaste
*say may a ka-**ee**-do el em-**pas**-tay*

This one hurts
Me duele ésta
*may **dwe**-lay es-ta*

FOR YOUR INFORMATION

Numbers

0	cero	***the**-ro*
1	uno	***oo**-no*
2	dos	*dos*
3	tres	*tres*
4	cuatro	***kwa**-tro*
5	cinco	***theen**-ko*
6	seis	*says*
7	siete	*see-**e**-tay*
8	ocho	***o**-cho*
9	nueve	***nwe**-bay*
10	diez	***dee**-eth*
11	once	***on**-thay*
12	doce	***do**-thay*

Numbers

13	trece *tre-thay*
14	catorce *ka-**tor**-thay*
15	quince ***keen**-thay*
16	dieciséis *dee-eth-ee-**says***
17	diecisiete *dee-eth-ee-see-**e**-tay*
18	dieciocho *dee-eth-ee-**o**-cho*
19	diecinueve *dee-eth-ee-**nwe**-bay*
20	veinte ***bain**-tay*
21	veintiuno *bain-tee-**oo**-no*
22	veintidós *bain-tee-**dos***
23	veintitrés *bain-tee-**tres***
24	veinticuatro *bain-tee-**kwa**-tro*
25	veinticinco *bain-tee-**theen**-ko*
26	veintiséis *bain-tee-**says***
27	veintisiete *bain-tee-see-**e**-tay*
28	veintiocho *bain-tee-**o**-cho*
29	veintinueve *bain-tee-**nwe**-bay*
30	treinta ***trayn**-ta*
40	cuarenta *kwa-**ren**-ta*

50	cincuenta *theen-kwen-ta*
60	sesenta *se-sen-ta*
70	setenta *se-ten-ta*
80	ochenta *o-chen-ta*
90	noventa *no-ben-ta*
100	cien, ciento *thee-en*, *thee-en-to*
200	doscientos *dos-thee-en-tos*
300	trescientos *tres-thee-en-tos*
400	cuatrocientos *kwa-tro-thee-en-tos*
500	quinientos *keen-yen-tos*
600	seiscientos *says-thee-en-tos*
700	setecientos *se-tay-thee-en-tos*
800	ochocientos *o-cho-thee-en-tos*
900	novecientos *no-bay-thee-en-tos*
1000	mil *meel*
2000	dos mil *dos meel*
3000	tres mil *tres meel*
4000	cuatro mil *kwa-tro meel*
1000000	un millón *oon mee-yon*

Ordinal numbers

1st	primero	*pree-**mair**-o*
2nd	segundo	*se-**goon**-do*
3rd	tercero	*tair-**thair**-o*
4th	cuarto	***kwar**-to*
5th	quinto	***keen**-to*
nth	enésimo	*e-**ne**-see-mo*

Fractions and percentages

a half	medio	***me**-dee-o*
a quarter	un cuarto	*oon **kwar**-to*
a third	un tercio	*oon **tair**-thee-o*
two thirds	dos tercios	*dos **tair**-thee-os*
10 %	diez por ciento	*dee-eth por thee-**en**-to*

Days

Sunday	domingo *do-**meen**-go*
Monday	lunes *loo-nes*
Tuesday	martes *mar-tes*
Wednesday	miércoles *mee-**air**-ko-les*
Thursday	jueves *hwe-bes*
Friday	viernes *bee-**air**-nes*
Saturday	sábado *sa-ba-do*

Dates

on Friday	el viernes *el bee-**air**-nes*
next Tuesday	el martes próximo *el **mar**-tes **prok**-see-mo*
last Tuesday	el martes pasado *el **mar**-tes pa-**sa**-do*
yesterday	ayer *a-**yair***
today	hoy *oy*
tomorrow	mañana *man-**ya**-na*
in June	en junio *en **hoo**-nee-o*

The seasons

July 7th el siete de julio *el see-**e**-tay day **hoo**-lee-o*

next week la semana que viene *la se-**ma**-na kay bee-**e**-nay*

last month el mes pasado *el mes pa-**sa**-do*

The seasons

spring primavera *pree-ma-**bair**-a*

summer verano *be-**ra**-no*

autumn otoño *o-**ton**-yo*

winter invierno *een-**byair**-no*

Times of the year

in spring en la primavera *en la pree-ma-**bair**-a*

in summer en el verano *en el be-**ra**-no*

in autumn en el otoño *en el o-**ton**-yo*

in winter en el invierno *en el een-**byair**-no*

Months

January	enero *e-nair-o*
February	febrero *fe-brair-o*
March	marzo *mar-tho*
April	abril *a-breel*
May	mayo *my-o*
June	junio *hoo-nee-o*
July	julio *hoo-lee-o*
August	agosto *a-go-sto*
September	setiembre *se-tee-em-bray*
October	octubre *ok-too-bray*
November	noviembre *nob-yem-bray*
December	diciembre *deeth-yem-bray*

Public holidays

When a holiday falls on a Tuesday or Thursday, the day between it and the weekend is usually declared a *puente* (bridge) and taken off as well.

Most shops, offices and museums are closed on the following days.

January 1, New Year's Day
Año Nuevo
an-yo nway-bo

January 6, Epiphany
Día de Reyes
dee-a day ray-es

Maundy Thursday
Jueves Santo
hwe-bes san-to

Good Friday
Viernes Santo
bee-air-nes san-to

May 1, May Day, Labour Day
Día del Trabajo
dee-a del tra-ba-ho

24 June, St John's Day
Día de San Juan Batista
dee-a day san hwan ba-tee-sta

Corpus Christi Day (2nd Thursday after Pentecost – late
  May or early June)
Corpus Christi
*kor-poos **kree**-stee*

25 July, St James's Day
Día de Santiago Apóstol
*dee-a day san-**tya**-go a-po-**stol***

15 August, Assumption
Asunción
*a-soon-**thyon***

12 October, Columbus Day
Día de la Hispanidad
*dee-a day la ee-spa-nee-**dad***

1 November, All Saints Day
Todos los Santos
*to-dos los **san**-tos*

6 December, Constitution Day
Día de la Constitución
*dee-a day la kon-stee-too-**thyon***

8 December, Immaculate Conception
Inmaculada Concepción
*een-ma-koo-**la**-da kon-thep-**thyon***

25 December, Christmas Day
Navidad
*na-bee-**dad***

Colours

black	**grey**
negro	gris
ne-gro	*grees*
blue	**orange**
azul	naranja
a-thool	*na-ran-ha*
brown	**pink**
marrón	rosa
ma-ron	*ro-sa*
cream	**purple**
crema	morado
kray-ma	*mo-ra-do*
fawn	**red**
beis	rojo
bays	*ro-ho*
gold	**silver**
dorado	plateado
do-ra-do	*pla-tay-a-do*
green	**tan**
verde	color canela
bair-day	*ko-lor ka-nay-la*

Common adjectives

white
blanco
blan-ko

yellow
amarillo
a-ma-ree-yo

Common adjectives

bad
malo
ma-lo

difficult
difícil
dee-fee-theel

beautiful
hermoso
air-mo-so

easy
fácil
fa-theel

big
grande
gran-day

fast
rápido
ra-pee-do

cheap
barato
ba-ra-to

good
bueno
bway-no

cold
frío
free-o

high
alto
al-to

expensive
caro
ka-ro

hot
caliente
ka-lee-en-tay

Signs and notices

little	**short**
poco	corto
po-ko	*kor*-to
long	**slow**
largo	lento
lar-go	*len*-to
new	**small**
nuevo	pequeño
nway-bo	pe-*ken*-yo
old	**ugly**
viejo	feo
bee-*ay*-ho	*fay*-o

Signs and notices (*see also* Road signs, page 111)

abierto	**agotado**
a-bee-*air*-to	a-go-*ta*-do
open	sold out
aduana	**agua potable**
a-*dwa*-na	*a*-gwa po-*ta*-blay
Customs	drinking water
agencia de viajes	**alarma de incendios**
a-*hen*-thee-a day bee-*a*-hes	a-*lar*-ma day een-*then*-dee-os
travel agency	fire alarm

232

ambulancia
am-boo-lan-thee-a
ambulance

aparcamiento sólo para residentes
a-par-ka-myen-to so-lo pa-ra re-see-den-tes
parking for residents only

área de fumadores
a-ray-a day foo-ma-do-res
smoking area

ascensor
as-then-sor
lift (elevator)

banco
ban-ko
bank

bienvenido
byen-be-nee-do
welcome

bomberos
bom-bair-os
fire brigade

caballeros
ka-ba-yair-os
gentlemen

cajero
ka-hair-o
cashier

caliente
ka-lee-en-tay
hot

camino particular
ka-mee-no par-tee-koo-lar
private road

carril de bicicleta
ka-reel day bee-thee-klay-ta
cycle path

cerrado
the-ra-do
closed

cerrado por la tarde
the-ra-do por la tar-day
closed in the afternoon

circule por la derecha
theer-koo-lay por la de-ray-cha
keep to the right

233

Signs and notices

colegio
co-le-hee-o
school

compartimento de fumadores
kom-par-tee-men-to day foo-ma-do-res
smoking compartment

cuidado
kwee-da-do
caution

cuidado con el perro
kwee-da-do kon el pe-ro
beware of the dog

desviación
des-bee-a-thyon
diversion

emergencia
e-mair-hen-thee-a
emergency

empujar
em-poo-har
push

entrada
en-tra-da
entrance

entrada gratuita
en-tra-da gra-twee-ta
no admission charge

entre sin llamar
en-tray seen ya-mar
enter without knocking

equipaje
e-kee-pa-hay
baggage

está prohibido hablar al conductor mientras circula
es-ta pro-ee-bee-do a-blar kon el kon-dook-tor myen-tras theer-koo-la
it is forbidden to speak to the driver while the bus is moving

frío
free-o
cold

234

Signs and notices

horario
o-ra-ree-o
timetable

hospital
os-pee-tal
hospital

información
een-for-ma-thyon
information

libre
lee-bray
vacant

lista de precios
lee-sta day pre-thee-os
price list

llame
ya-may
ring

llame por favor
ya-may por fa-bor
please ring

llegadas
ye-ga-das
arrivals

no entrar
no en-trar
no entry

no pisar el césped
no pee-sar el thes-ped
keep off the grass

no tocar
no to-kar
do not touch

ocupado
o-koo-pa-do
occupied

oferta especial
o-fair-ta es-peth-yal
special offer

oficina de objetos perdidos
o-fee-thee-na day ob-he-tos pair-dee-dos
lost property office

papelera
pa-pe-lair-a
litter

235

Signs and notices

peligro
pe-lee-gro
danger

peligro de incendio
pe-lee-gro day een-then-dee-o
danger of fire

peligro de muerte
pe-lee-gro day mwair-tay
danger of death

permitido sólo para…
pair-mee-tee-do so-lo pa-ra…
allowed only for…

policia
po-lee-thee-a
police

prohibida la entrada
pro-ee-bee-da la en-tra-da
no trespassing

prohibido asomarse
pro-ee-bee-do a-so-mar-say
do not lean out

prohibido el paso
pro-ee-bee-do el pa-so
no thoroughfare

prohibido fumar
pro-ee-bee-do foo-ma
no smoking

prohibido hacer fotos
pro-ee-bee-do a-thair fo-tos
no picture taking

rebajas
re-ba-has
sale

recuerdos
re-kwair-dos
souvenirs

reservado
re-sair-ba-do
reserved

salida
sa-lee-da
exit

salida de emergencia
sa-lee-da day e-mair-hen-thee-a
emergency exit

salidas
sa-lee-das
departures

se alquila
*say al-**kee**-la*
to let (for hire)

se vende
*say **ben**-day*
for sale

señoras
*sen-**yo**-ras*
ladies

sólo empleados
*so-lo em-play-**a**-dos*
employees only

sólo para uso externo
*so-lo **pa**-ra **oo**-so ek-**stair**-no*
for external use only

teléfono
*te-**le**-fo-no*
telephone

timbre de alarma
***teem**-bray day a-**lar**-ma*
communication cord

tirar
*tee-**rar***
pull

veneno
*be-**nay**-no*
poison

venta de liquidación
ben**-ta day lee-kee-da-**thyon
closing down sale

IN AN EMERGENCY

What to do

Spain has three police forces. The Guardia Civil, who wear green uniforms, deal with law enforcement on the roads and in rural areas. They do not enjoy a great reputation for helpfulness. The Policía Local, who wear blue and white uniforms, patrol within towns and can be approached about any difficulties. The Policía Nacional, who wear blue uniforms, guard public buildings and in all substantial towns man the *comisaría* (police station), where crimes may be reported. In addition, the autonomous communities of the Basque Country, Catalonia, Galicia and Valencia have their own police forces. Telephone 091 for the Policía Nacional, 092 for the Policía Local.

If you suffer a loss or theft, report the incident to the police and obtain a copy of the report. If your passport is stolen or lost, inform the nearest British Consulate so that they can issue you with temporary papers.

For assistance with fires, refer to local directories or call the operator.

Call — the fire brigade
Llame — a los bomberos
*ya-may — a los bom-**bair**-os*

— the police
— a la policía
— *a la po-lee-thee-a*

—an ambulance
— a una ambulancia
— *a oo-na am-boo-lan-thee-a*

Get a doctor
Busque a un médico
boos-kay a oon me-dee-ko

There is a fire
Hay un incendio
eye oon en-then-dee-o

Where is — the British consulate?
¿Dónde está — el consulado británico?
don-day es-ta — el kon-soo-la-do bree-ta-nee-ko

— the police station?
— la comisaría de policía?
— *la ko-mee-sa-ree-a day po-lee-thee-a*